THE HOT SUN OF AFRICA

CALIBER
BOOKS

Also from ALAN CAILLOU

CABOT CAIN Series
    Assault on Kolchak
    Assault on Ming
    Assault on Loveless
    Assault on Fellawi
    Assault on Agathon
    Assault on Almata

TOBIN'S WAR Series
    Dead Sea Submarine
    Terror in Rio
    Congo War Cry
    Afghan Assault
    Swamp War
    Death Charge
    The Garonsky Missile

MIKE BENASQUE Series
    The Plotters
    Marseilles
    Who'll Buy My Evil
    Diamonds Wild

IAN QUAYLE Series
    A League of Hawks
    The Sword of God

DEKKER'S DEMONS Series
    Suicide Run
    Blood Run

The Charge of the Light Brigade
A Journey to Orassia

Rogue's Gambit
Cairo Cabal
Bichu the Jaguar
The Walls of Jolo
The Hot Sun of Africa
The Cheetahs
Joshua's People
Mindanao Pearl
Khartoum
South from Khartoum
Rampage
The World is 6 Feet Square
The Prophetess
House on Curzon Street

THE HOT SUN OF AFRICA

PART ONE

The Land

CHAPTER 1

When the ship steamed slowly into the blue-green harbor with its red roofs and whitewashed buildings, as it slowly entered the most beautiful harbor in the world, where the sky was bursting with the heat and the water boiling under the searching bow, Tabor lay back in the deck chair and left the hawking to the others, to those who lined the decks and watched the *'ngalaus* gliding by in absolute silence, their outriggers cutting into the water where the shark and the barracuda hunted among the floating garbage from the ships.

It was new, and strange, and full of unexpected delights, and he wanted not to see them coming, but to wake up one day and find himself among them as though they had surrounded him all his life; he wanted to find himself suddenly, more abruptly, in the new environment, to make it part of himself more completely, so that he would be only half conscious, as though in a self-imposed coma, of the changed and still changing world that was gently enfolding.

He wanted to wake up one morning in a strange place and say: *I have lived here all my life. This is my home. I do not know any other world.*

When a shadow fell across his chair he looked up with a touch of irritation, and Weldon was there; Weldon was another passenger, a man he did not like, a man with white flesh that had been burned bright red by the sun and who wore sandals on his blistered feet and three cameras around his scrawny neck.

Weldon said: "Aren't you going to watch?"

Tabor shook his head and closed his eyes, and Weldon said

curiously: "You aim to stay here long? Going on safari?"

It was an effort to open his eyes again. He said slowly: "Just thought I'd look around for a while."

"You were wise not to bring Mrs. Tabor. There *is* a Mrs. Tabor, isn't there?"

Tabor said shortly: "I'm traveling alone."

Weldon nodded eagerly. "Sure, I know what it's like. My wife wanted to stay home too; hell, she says they don't even have Kleenex out here." He leaned over the rail and watched the water for a while and said happily: "You know, my wife's one of those women...her only experience of exotica was when she tasted a Spanish omelet in a drugstore; she didn't like it. What's a woman like that going to do in Africa, can you tell me that? So I said, 'Sure honey, you stay home, I'll bring you back a Masai for a houseboy.'" When Tabor closed his eyes and did not answer, he said suspiciously: "But it's your first time out here? You been here before?"

"My first time."

"And you don't want to watch the ship coming in? They say the harbor's full of sharks, big as a submarine. Octopus, too. I wonder if they go diving for pennies, like they do in Port Said? You think they do?"

"Maybe."

Weldon pulled a piece of skin from his burnt nose and said: "Well, see you ashore, I guess. Maybe we can get together for a drink, how'd that be?"

"Sure."

When he opened his eyes again, Weldon was gone. He wished he had not mentioned his wife.

It was all so far away now, in time and in place, and the efforts to forget were budding slowly, coming to fruition so slowly that sometimes he had to force himself to forget, knowing that he always wanted to forget what was unpleasant and to remember only the good things; and if this was wrong, it was none the less the way he wanted it to be, for there was so little time to search...

With all the imaginings in the world, it was impossible to put the past glibly behind him. There was always the shadow there, of her and of his guilt, cast across the years behind him, seeming to twist

6

itself to cover also the future, if he would let it. He could not entirely put the thought of her away from him, knowing that mingled with his guilt there was still some sort of longing for her, even though in the past few months he had grown not to love her anymore, not even to want her.

There were the long white gloves and the elegant dresses, and the cool shadows under the Connecticut trees, and the sound of a pinto's hooves over the turf; and that was all that was left of her. That, and the shame.

Thinking of her again, angry with the disruption of his tranquility, he could not sit still. He got up quickly and joined the other passengers and stared with them at the nearing shoreline, at the palm trees bent over the water, at the fishing nets held up with old oil drums, and at the black, half-naked children playing at the water's edge where the channel cut in close to the sandy shore.

An old *dhow*, the five small windows in its prow proclaiming its ancient origins in the cool bays of Portugal, was swaying gently at anchor by a wooden wharf, and a white-bearded Arab on board was squatting in the crude head which jutted out over the sea. An African in a narrow outrigger was hauling in a long black rope, and his tiny craft was piled high with lobster baskets. A sunken cruiser (was it German?) was jutting rustily up at the side of the harbor's channel, tilted crazily, the water gently lapping at its toppled smokestack. And on the northern bank a sandy track, unpaved, led to a small village of rickety houses where he could see chickens and goats wandering aimlessly in the hot dry shade of a giant acacia tree.

It was as far removed from Connecticut as anything in the world.

He was a big man, standing six feet four in his socks and weighing in at well over two hundred pounds; his shoulders were huge and his forearm was like the branch of an oak. There had been a time when muscular efficiency had seemed the answer to the restlessness that perturbed him, but that was behind him now. His forty-five years, and the cessation of most of his physical activity over the past twenty, had brought him the beginnings of a paunch—the price, he called it, of sudden wealth. There had been a time, too, after the difficult beginnings, when the answer had seemed to lie in an expansion of his environment, when all that was necessary was to broaden the horizon, to branch out, as it were, into a wider world that was far from the rigid confines of a restricting society, to spread his intellectual tentacles to embrace all that which once had seemed so far away and so infinitely unattainable.

There had been the abortive search for fulfillment on the Venezuelan ranch; and the brief period in the Texas oil field, cut short because *she* wanted him back... And at last the final, the definite step, a fine old villa in Italy where there was all the elegance in the world and where *she* could play the grand lady... It was a villa of awesome architecture and a startling, almost unreal view across the bluest water in the world.

The definite step, he had called it, *the step that can at the same time give me the embrace of the unknown and leave you the constancy of the elegance;* and for a while it had worked.

He stared into the water, as startlingly blue here as it had been in Italy, blue and overpowering and part of that other world that he could not escape from. Even the quiet was part of that world, and the past was more vivid than the present.

The awesome architecture of the old Italian *palazzo* was bright behind him, shining in the sunlight as the old columns had always been meant to shine, as a testimony to man's love of ordered grace. Its ornate pillars caught the sunlight, and their marble shimmer was covered with blue and green wisteria, with green and bright red bougainvillea, and with yellow clusters of sweet-smelling honeysuckle, the scent of it reaching out even down here on the beach and bringing them both the richness of its fragrance.

Looking up at the sky, his bronzed body stretched lazily on the sand beside her, he was saying: "Environment, honey, a man makes his own. You think it's the other way around?"

Beyond the beach, beyond the *palazzo,* the steep hill rose sharply, white sand covered with tall dark pines where the sharp brown cones lay scattered among the needles.

The smile did not leave her lips as she turned to look at him. "You're more arrogant than I thought you were. And even if you are right, our environment is not here, it is in Connecticut, darling, except the little piece of it we brought along with us."

"Packed in a suitcase?"

She touched her forehead delicately. "Up here, that's where our environment belongs. Have you never heard of heritage?"

He felt a touch of impatience with her. (And he was beginning to feel it more often now.) He said slowly: "Perhaps my heritage is older than yours."

He hated the little separations that came between them, hated them only because they were small.

She put out a hand and touched him, and he looked at the long, immaculate fingernails and he said gently: "It's just not as firmly rooted, that's all."

"A loner."

"Something like that. Till you came along."

"There's something rather pathetic about a lonely man."

"Lone. Not lonely. There's one hell of a difference."

"And you think you'll find some consolation for it...here? In this?"

She stretched a negligent hand behind her towards the villa and the garden where the geraniums were blooming.

He shrugged. "If you don't like it, I wish you'd said so earlier."

"It's an awful place."

He was genuinely shocked. He sat up and looked at her and said incredulously: "You can't really mean that."

She said again, carefully: "It's an awful place."

He was aghast at the unexpectedness of it. For more than a month he had searched, looking for just the right place, for just the right touch of grandeur to satisfy her and yet remain within the bounds of his own approval. It was a fine old building, gleaming white, with orderly flower beds and ornamental hedges, and a fountain that made soft noises by the cypress trees. The steps wound up and up and up from the beach, leading, it seemed, to an eminence of privilege, to a plateau of quality and seclusion that surely would satisfy her completely; it was a villa that seemed to state its own excellence in noble phrases, and there was no line in it that was not...*patrician*. The tall hills behind it shielded it from the road, as

9

though for decades it had lain here, hidden, gently mourning the passing of an ancient aristocracy, waiting to be used again, waiting to hold its great beauty around... anyone who could stand for a while and catch his breath at its marvelous symmetry.

He had bought it on the spur of the moment, gladly, and he had sent a delighted cable, and she had come and looked it over and had said, murmuring: "It's almost insolently dramatic, isn't it?"

He looked quickly over his shoulder at the beautiful lines of the white building, then back at her long cool body, spread out elegantly, legs crossed, on the bright blue towel, just so; the straps of her green costume were immaculately in place. Her thighs were long and slim, her breasts small and tight, her stomach taut; somewhere in the delicate arch of her eyebrows and the hollows under the cheekbones, there was reflected a trace of some remote Italianate strain that sharpened her beauty. It was a face that held its aloof excellence at whatever angle, a face which painters would stare at and sculptors long to touch. It was a cool self-assured face, immeasurably controlled and sure of its own loveliness.

He said: "Hell, if I thought you really meant that... I was so sure you'd fall in love with it... That's eighty thousand bucks down the drain."

That damned smile was still there, and the lift of the shoulder was so slight he might have imagined it.

"Not really. I'm sure you'll be very happy here."

A touch of ice seemed to tickle his spine. When she did not speak, he said, controlling his voice carefully: "Is there something you want to tell me? If there is..."

"Then lie down, you're keeping the sun off me."

Obediently, he lay back in the sand, waiting.

She said without emotion, "I'm going to leave you, I'm afraid."

A bird swooped down and cast a sudden, fleeting shadow, and then wheeled away out above the water. He thrust the brutal shock of it away from him, sat up again, his heart pounding, and wrapped his arms around his knees. Far out to sea he could distinguish the white and gray bulk of a small steamer, the smoke standing above it in an upright, motionless column.

He played with the sand for a while, dribbling it through his fingers, steadying their trembling, and said at last: "When?"

"Tonight."

"Who is it? Harry?"

"No." There was a moment of uneasiness in her voice, a small triumph for him. "Someone you don't know, you've never even met him."

Was that the truth, or a hopeful shield for his best friend? He said tightly: "I'm bound to hear about it, you may as well tell me who he is."

She did not answer, and he looked at her (marveling at his own coolness), and said, "All right, I'll give you a divorce, if that's what you want. Does Jacobson know?" Jacobson was the lawyer.

"Of course not. If I have to hurt you... at least you have the right to be the first one to know."

He said laconically: "Thanks."

"I'm sorry, truly sorry."

"I'll tell Jacobson to get in touch with you."

She sat up now and looked at him, faintly troubled. "You're not fighting me. Why? Did you expect it?"

He took a deep breath. "No, not really. But there aren't many things I'll fight for, and you're not one of them."

He saw real hatred in her eyes now, but she lay back on the sand and stared up at the sky, and he looked with longing at her great beauty and knew that he wanted her more than he had ever wanted anything on earth. He looked at the long lines of her body and at the cool alabaster of her skin, and suddenly there was nothing but loathing for her, and he reached down and put his hands at her throat and shouted, "I ought to choke the life out of you...!"

He heard her scream, and the violent abnegation of her deadly calm was a triumph for him, a triumph that seemed to make it more essential now to choke the life right out of her.

He could not understand where the sudden violence came from, but he did not question it; he used it without stopping to think, feeling the exquisite softness her throat under his hands, feeling only soft flesh between his crushing fingers.

She arched her body in pain, and the long legs thrashed out, and she clutched at the heavy, masculine wrists, and her breast was tight against him as she struggled; her body was lithe, writhing, unbelievably supple as she tried to twist away from him, and he rolled with her, rolling over and over, feeling her body underneath him as he had so often (and so incompletely) felt it before, as he pulled her to the edge of the water and thrust her face into the surf. Her legs kept thrashing as she tried to scream, and then...

The passion in him shocked him, and there was shock, too, at the sudden terror in her eyes, and it seemed that the world was swinging violently around him, as though he were drunk, and he threw himself back from her so that he hurt himself when he hit the sand, and he struggled to his feet and said, infinitely appalled: "My God, my God, I tried to kill you."

One hand was at her throat, as the water lapped at her thighs, and her lovely face was drawn and white with pain. A shoulder strap had fallen down so that one breast was quite exposed, but she did not heed it; he did not know how long, or how violently, she had struggled under his powerful hands. There was a great red sore under her chin, as though he had almost torn the skin away from her.

She stared at him in an astonishment that was somehow ridiculous, an astonishment that was greater than the sudden access of fear. He knew that his own face was white, too, and he said, "My God, what was I going to do...?"

Very slowly, she got to her feet, went and picked up the bright blue towel, and methodically began to fold it. He could see that she was trembling, and when he reached out and touched her, she did not move; it was like touching a marble statue. Then she picked up the bright straw bag he had bought her from a street vendor, and walked stiffly, silently, up the path to the villa.

He stayed there for a long, long time, savoring the strangeness, wondering about the unexpected violence that had come over him. He looked out at the sea and said over and over again: "I don't believe it, I don't believe it..." He could still see the savage bruises at her throat, and he looked at his hands in revulsion; and he felt something like fear.

When it was dark, a light went on in the upstairs suite which they used as dressing rooms, and a little while later he heard the sound of a car drawing up outside the front door—the smooth, authoritative purr of an expensive European automobile. It purred there for a while, and then some doors slammed and the sound faded away and he knew that she was gone, forever.

The light stayed on, mocking him with its emptiness, and he went into the water and swam for half an hour, and then he walked down the cold beach until the moon had gone down and there was only darkness all around him. The gritty sand between his toes bit deeply into his flesh.

And he knew that as long as he lived, the shocking memory of the violence that was in his hands would remain with him.

When the ship docked, Willis was there to meet him, a white-haired man with a pleasant, affable expression and an air of casual authority, an elderly man whose world was ordered and acceptable because he had helped to make it that way; there was something in the quick competence of his movements that seemed to say: *Here, we are secure, we know which way we are heading, and our world has been fashioned in the way we like it.*

To the casual observer (to the Weldons, Tabor thought), the relaxed and easy courtesy was all that could be seen, but there was something else there, deep under the surface.

Feeling the firm, friendly grip, Tabor said: "So you got my wire."

"Of course. The day of the cleft stick is a long way past, Mr. Tabor. If you give me your baggage checks I'll have the boys take care of it for you." He turned to the young man who stood beside him, a good-looking youngster in his early twenties. "Mr. Cassel, my assistant, Mr. Tabor." He grinned quickly and said: "One of the best shots in the business, Mr. Tabor. And we've laid on a good safari for you. First, down to the Rufiji. Is that suitable?"

"Sure. You're the boss."

"Your baggage?"

Tabor kicked at a small suitcase on the deck. "Just the one case."

Willis raised an eyebrow. "But...you must have more than that..."

Patting his wallet Tabor said: "In my pocket. Travelers cheques. Thought I'd buy what I need."

"No guns?"

They say the gunsmiths here are pretty good."

Astonished, Willis said, "First time I've had a client with less than fifty pieces of luggage." He added mildly: "Most of which has to be left behind. The rules are pretty strict here...the guns they allow you to use..."

The African porters were swarming aboard, pushing about violently, their sweaty bodies shining, their bare feet padding along the deck, their white teeth gleaming happily.

Looking at them, marveling at their irrepressible laughter, Tabor said: "It's a new world for me, Mr. Willis. Somehow, I think I'm going to like it."

"Good. The better you like it, the longer you'll stay. We'll see if we can get you some really good trophies."

"Just let's take what comes our way, shall we?"

There was a moment of hesitation, of distrust almost, but Willis nodded cheerfully. "All right."

"Main thing is... Hell, all I want is to get out into the bush, see what it has to offer that we don't have back home."

"And that's plenty. A few days in town to get your equipment. Have you ever hunted before?"

"Went after some kodiak once. Didn't get near them."

"Well, we'll do better with the lions."

"And the crocodiles?"

Willis looked at him curiously. "Yes, I wondered about that. Your letter...it seemed somehow an odd choice. Most people would rather go after lion, leopard, elephant...the big game. What made you mention the crocodile?"

"I heard they're classed as vermin. I don't like parasites, Mr. Willis. Maybe I'll feel better shooting them."

Willis looked quickly at Cassel and said: "Well, the Rufiji it is. This time of the year the crocodiles cover the swamps, packed like sardines in a can."

And later that night, while Tabor was taking a shower in the small old-fashioned hotel with its creeper-covered verandas, Cassel said happily, "We've got a client who likes to stamp out vermin. Answer the question there, if you can."

Willis snapped his fingers for the barman. He said slowly: "You should read the New York papers once in a while. His wife ran off with a fortune-hunter, and I'm afraid... He just might try to take it out on the animals. It's not unusual." Unthinking, he added: "A man with wife trouble shouldn't hunt; it's not fair, is it?"

For a moment, Cassel looked at him with a touch of anger. But Willis was leaning across the bar and reaching for the lemons, paying him no attention at all.

The younger man turned away, his good humor gone, and said sourly, "Any man with a wife shouldn't hunt."

There was almost a moment of antagonism, but not quite. Willis covered up quickly. Smiling, he said, "If you get hurt by an animal, you can always hit back, can't you?"

Two weeks later, their first hunt together began.

As far as you could see, the eerie white mist hung motionless over the deadly swamp. The great dark masses that were the mangrove trees stood out in untidy asymmetry through the pale mist, and sometimes, as the dugouts glided silently along, they could see the gnarled stumps that stuck up from the black water, like knobby fists reaching up out of the slime.

For more than a week they had moved south and inland, pushing the truck forward until it would go no farther but sank up to its axle in the beginnings of the quagmire, and then they had sent the boys on ahead to make camp while they had moved on in the dugouts with a single gunbearer at a more leisurely pace. The insects had hummed around them like quick-moving feather dusters, in mobile clouds that moved with them as they splashed through the mud.

Once, Willis said to Tabor: "You think it's worth it? If you want to go back..."

Tabor had answered gruffly; "Let's push on."

When they reached dry land again, Willis shot a *kudu*, and the boy skinned it expertly and cooked the fillet for them over a twig fire, hoisting the rest of the meat on his bloody shoulders and trudging on with it happily. He was a tall, well-built Nandi from up North, a stolid, silent man with coal-black skin and three fingers missing from his left hand after a careless encounter with a wild boar, and his name was Adoula.

He carried the three-hundred-pound carcass effortlessly, and at the end of the day, miraculously, the camp was there where it was supposed to be, with the porters still coming in from the swamp villages, and the dugouts they would use already lined up at the edge of the river.

The porters were squat, muscular men with sharply filed teeth; Tabor looked at them curiously and said: "Cannibals? I don't believe it."

Willis nodded. "They were once. They still are, some of them. The young men don't file their teeth anymore, they want to show they've given up the old ways. But once in a while, when there's no meat... And even then, only their enemies."

"A good way to get rid of a body."

Tabor laughed suddenly, and Willis said cheerfully: "I'd never have believed you could really enjoy this."

"Like I said, a new world." Practicing his new Swahili phrases, he turned to one of the porters and said: "*Wapi Adoula?*"

He had shown an unexpected aptitude with the language. Willis had said, smiling, "If you don't know the word, then use the English and add a vowel, chances are you'll be pretty close." Tabor had learned that Swahili was a lingua franca, no more than a second language for most of the tribesmen who spoke their own dialects and could not converse, except with difficulty, with men who came from other tribal lands, and he'd wondered, startled, how long it would take this world to gather to itself the cohesion of the one he had left...

The porter got slowly to his feet, fingering his face with thin hands that were like the bones of a mummy. He thought for a while and then pointed with his long stick. "Out there," he said. "*K-u-u-u-l-e...*" drawing the word out long, because, while *kule* meant "over there," the longer he took over saying the word the farther away it meant. His ribs threw dark shadows over the gray ash on his torso, gray ash which had been plastered on with urine to keep the insects away, and he scratched at the lice on his body, searching for

16

inspiration, wanting to say something else in Swahili (which was a foreign tongue to him) to prove to his fellows that he knew other languages as well as his local dialect, and that he was therefore a clever man who could converse with those who came from distant places.

He remembered one of the words, and said, beaming: "*Mzuri, mzuri*," meaning "good," and hoping that the white man would realize he meant that everything was good in the world now that he was working and would be paid for his work. And then he squatted down again, nodded wisely at the others, filled his long clay pipe with a mixture of dried leaves and cow dung, lit it with a stick from the fire, and puffed on it contentedly.

The twilight hung in the air for a moment or two, and then suddenly it was gone and there was only darkness.

Now the noise was intolerable. The crickets screeched deafeningly, the toads croaked their unbelievable bass-baritones, the insects hummed, and the birds called loudly to one another, filling the swamp with a monstrous cacophony that seemed to smother them, embracing, like the immensity of the distance, the whole of the world.

The tent had been set up on a dry path of ground under a mangrove tree—so small a patch they had to step carefully to avoid slipping into the mud—and its pressure lamp cast a yellow glow over the crowding mosquitoes that were trying to force a way through the nets over its door; the air was heavy with the smoke of the fires that were meant to keep them away.

They had rubbed their bodies with citronella oil, but Willis said: "Gin's the only thing, really. Let them bite you, and if you take enough gin you won't get malaria." He took the big flashlight and shone it across the water and said, "Out there, a few hundred yards up the channel, all the crocodile in the world." He listened for a while to the monotonous chant of the porters squatting around the fires and said: "They're singing about you." The atonal chant was a melancholy dirge that suddenly changed to a beat of triumph, a war song of victory, and Willis, listening, said: "The village headman lost his third wife last week; a croc took her while she went down to the water to clean the cooking pot, and they're telling how you've come to kill their enemy."

The headman had come with the porters, a fat, jovial man in a bright feather headdress, who interspersed every guttural comment with a great bellow of laughter.

Tabor said: "Last week? He didn't seem to be in mourning, did he?"

Willis shrugged. "With the money he gets for the porters he can buy a dozen wives. And the crocodiles are too much a part of their everyday existence to worry about. Children, women, the old men...anyone who can't move smartly enough or hasn't got his wits about him... The village lost eighteen people last year. They drag the bodies down under the water, stuff them into a cave, and come back for the meal when they start to decay. And still, the women wash at the river, the children swim there... They never seem to learn."

He snapped off the light as Adoula came silently beside them and said: "*Tayari, Bwana*, we are ready."

"Two men to a boat, no more."

Adoula hesitated. "The boats are longer, *Bwana*. Better take four."

"All right. But good men, all of them."

"The best there are."

Adoula's voice, gentle and deep-throated, sounded the words as though Swahili were a foreign language to him too, knowing that the *Bwana* understood it better than he did, but that the new white man, the client with all the money, wanted to learn it as well. He wore khaki shorts and a singlet, with khaki puttees and bare feet, because he was proud of the fact that he had once been a warden in the National Park and liked to show off all that was left of his uniform; even here, after the long trek, his shorts were starched, clean, immaculately ironed with the heavy charcoal iron he always carried. His chest was as broad as a beer barrel, and his stomach muscles were taut and hard.

His white teeth gleaming in the darkness, he said: "I think there will be much work for the skinners tonight."

Tabor had gone for his new rifle, and now he came back, moving silently, slipping a flashlight in the pre-aligned clips that lay along the barrel. He aimed it carefully at the black bulk of a mangrove trunk and carefully adjusted the screws till the sights were lined up in the middle of the round white beam, and then he focused the flashlight carefully will the circle shrank small and smaller, and still the sights were dead center.

He said: "About fifty yards?"

Willis nodded approvingly. "Any closer, you're in trouble. Better let me take a look at it."

Tabor, without a word, handed him the rifle, and Willis checked the alignment of the flashlight, checked the bolt, checked the magazine, checked the sights, and handed it back.

He noticed the look on Tabor's face and said mildly, "Well, I'm sorry, but if there's anything wrong, I'm the one who's responsible."

"Sure."

"After all, it's your first hunt. And the faster you learn the more you're liable to forget."

Tabor grunted. "Maybe that's my only vice; I don't forget, ever."

He snapped off the light, strapped his leggings tightly over his boots, and stepped gingerly into the narrow dugout, trying it for size, staring at it almost angrily as though it were deliberately designed to thwart him. It was a long log of wood, hollowed out with knife and fire, no more than sixteen inches wide, but twelve or more feet long.

The paddlers sat in the center, their narrow haunches confined by the gunwales, their bony knees up-thrust, their short paddles ready. The boat seemed incredibly fragile.

"Remember," Willis said. "If you sit down, don't try to get right in, put one cheek on each side and watch your balance. And, when you fire, for God's sake make sure you shoot straight ahead. You fire a couple of inches to one side and the recoil will turn it over, no trouble at all, just spin it over like a cork. There's no centerboard, nothing like that, and the weight has to be bang in the center. Shift the weight a couple of inches, that's all, and the boat goes over."

"You call this piece of goddam piping a boat?"

"And it will tip over if you as much as sneeze. If you twist your body—"

"I know, you told me."

Willis said calmly, "And I'll tell you again. You tip the boat over, and you'll have fifty of them after you like a fleet of outboard motor boats, another tasty dish, and I'll have lost a client. I'll be right behind you, but if you do go over, swim straight for the shore. Keep moving straight because I'll be doing some pretty rapid firing. Just remember one thing; down here, we're a long way from the regular hunting grounds, and there's just a chance they may not be as scared by the shooting as they would be elsewhere. And that means they just might come for you. If they do, I'll have all my work cut out."

"Okay, okay, I get the message."

Two of the Africans, the black water lapping at their legs and washing away the gray ash, gently slid the dugout into the deep water.

Tabor turned his head to watch Willis, and someone shouted his alarm as the *'ngalau* tipped dangerously to one side. For a moment, it wobbled perilously as the Africans steadied it, and then it was smoothly, silently moving on a black sheet of glass that was spotted with bright clumps of green vegetation, the ripples ahead of it moving away in gentle cuneiform. He heard Willis say to Adoula: "Follow us along the bank. If a boat goes over, keep firing into the water as fast as you can."

Tabor guessed he had handed Adoula the third rifle, an old Army three-0-three, but he did not dare turn his head again to look, and in a moment the second *'ngalau*, with Willis aboard, was gliding along beside and slightly behind him. The two slim craft looked like sticks on the water that had dropped from an overhanging branch and were floating silently with the current.

Very gently he raised his rifle to his shoulder, feeling the reflex of the movement in the dugout, practicing it, forcing an unaccustomed care on himself. And when they were in midstream, he began to see the crocodiles on the other bank, packed tight in a dense mass, slowly heaving as they moved.

He said quietly: "Can we start shooting?"

Willis switched on his flashlight. "Whenever you're ready."

The paddlers on one side stopped working and let the craft glide silently on towards the bank under its own momentum, and Tabor switched on the light, aimed the circle at a long triangular snout, found the spherical gray bulge of the eye, and fired. He was astonished at the sound of the report in the darkness, and gratified to find that the boat did not tip.

He waited a moment and the crocodile had not moved, and he said, surprised: "I missed? I was right on target."

But Willis said: "A good shot, he's dead. Right through the eye. Take the big one ahead of you.

The others, packed so densely they overlapped each other, had not stirred. The dugout was pulling around to the delicate touch of a single paddle, and again he found a long gray snout, the malevolent eye staring straight at him, and when he fired he saw the skin fly off and with a flurry of water the croc was in the mud, swishing away fast with a lash of its violent tail.

Willis shouted: "You got him, the boys will fish him out. Keep at it..."

He fired again and again and again, remembering to keep his aiming straight ahead, and cursing when the dugout did not move around fast enough to permit a dead-ahead line of fire, and soon the water was white with the thrashing tails, and the marsh was alive with the sound of the gun.

Willis thought, admiring the ease and proficiency: *He does it well because he loves it, or he loves it because he does it well. Which is it, I wonder...?* He saw that the crew were working well, swinging the dugout around in a tight circle, keeping an even keel; it was like shooting ducks in a gallery, and he called out: "Where did you learn to shoot like that?"

But Tabor was busy working the bolt, slipping in a new cartridge, firing again... It seemed that the rifle, held rigorously, with marvelous discipline, on its proper line, did not move at all, but that the crocodiles themselves were slowly swinging around into its murderous range. The bellows of rage mingled with the sharp noises of the shots, and the water was alive with the fury of them.

And then, the sound Willis had been half-expecting came suddenly upon them. It was the dull thud of an angry snout crashing into the side of the dugout.

He saw Tabor throw up his arms to save his balance, and saw the rifle go swinging into the swamp, and he saw the boys leap for their lives as the craft went over, and then Tabor was in the water, too, standing there with a look of shocked surprise on his face, up to his waist in wet black mud, staring at the Africans who were already

21

thrashing at the slime with their arms, half-swimming, half-wading, forcing their thin bodies towards the safety of the shore.

He heard Willis call, quite calmly: "Get to the shore, I'll cover you..." and he thrust his bulk against the confining mud and began the long wade across the stinking blackness that was the surface of the swamp, swinging his powerful shoulders against the sludge. His feet squelched as they sucked out of the mud, and the mud pulled at him, seeking to drag him under. He saw a crocodile coming at him, and there was a moment of alarm, and then he heard the two quick shots that Willis pumped into it, and it was gone.

He saw Adoula, a dark shadow in the darkness, firing shot after shot into the water close beside him, scaring them away, and then the first of the paddlers had reached the shore and was showing his white teeth and driving away the moment of panic by the huge humor he found in the spectacle of Tabor's discomfort.

There was a moment more of giant tails thrashing, and then they were gone. The swamp was suddenly empty of them. One of the Africans, close to the shore, turned back now as Adoula shouted to him, and reached for the overturned canoe, pulling it towards him and yelling at the others (all of them laughing now) to help him. Strong black hands pulled him ashore, and he stumbled onto the bank and fell exhausted to the ground.

Then Willis drifted in with his *'ngalau* and stepped lightly ashore and said, "Well, are we all right?"

Panting hard, Tabor looked around at the empty, silent river, and said: "Where the hell did they all go?"

Willis grinned at him. "A few shots in the water... They're in their secret caverns, waiting, hiding out like any other animal that meets his betters." He held out a hand and pulled Tabor to his feet and said reprovingly: "You lost your rifle."

Struggling up, Tabor said: "The hell with it. But I got nine of them."

"Eight. One of them was only wounded. He'll probably get away. As soon as it's daylight, the boys will get the others. And there'll be quite a feast. Eight less of their enemies, eight less to take their wives and their children. That makes you something like a god for them. How does it feel?"

Tabor looked at him somberly. "Not as good as I thought it would. And I could do with some whiskey."

Tabor joked about the lost rifle as they drank their whiskeys by the fire, but deep inside him there was a kind of resentment, well repressed, because Willis, the expert, found it amusing too.

And from then on, there was a great determination that it would not happen again. It became almost a symbol of his power, because he knew that out here, in his new world, with a rifle in his hand he could do almost anything at all.

CHAPTER 2

The main street of the little town ran in a short straight line, flanked by whitewashed stores, some plaster-peeled, some crumbling, some showing the bright lights of kerosene pressure lamps and some glowing dimly with the pale glow of unshaded electric bulbs. At the all-night gas station on the corner where the date palms were, the African watchman lay wrapped in a blanket, fast asleep under the overhang of the door to the garage; if a customer should call, he would rub the sleep from his tired old eyes, grin happily, and go and find the Indian owner.

The rains had come that night, breaking over the town in a sudden deluge that had the streets ankle-deep in swirling, muddy water within the first three minutes. It rained so hard that the sound of the drops on the corrugated iron roof of the restaurant was like the sound of too-near drums; it seemed the roof would collapse under the relentless hammering.

When Tabor walked into the little Greek restaurant he saw Willis at a table with a woman and two men. The white hunter spotted him instantly and waved.

Tabor sauntered over to their table, and Willis said: "Mr. Tabor, fast getting to be the best shot in the Territory, Mrs. Marion Cassel." He shook hands with Tabor and said: "You remember Cassel, he used to work for me?"

Tabor nodded. He said gravely: "A real pleasure, Mrs. Cassel." Her beauty was breathtaking. He looked at her hands which were lying on the table. They were long and supple, well kept, and strong too.

"And Mr. Markos, Mr. Papadopoulos, Mr. Tabor. Sit down, we're just having some ozou. Have you had dinner?"

"Sure, six o'clock."

Marion Cassel said: "You don't really eat dinner at six in the evening, do you?" She looked at the small gold watch that lay on the table and said: "Half past nine."

Tabor said: "You leave that lying there, you're liable to forget it." He looked at Marion's slim wrist and said, smiling: "Don't you like to wear a wristwatch, ma'am?"

She said: "For God's sake don't call me ma'am," and he grinned at her quickly and sat down.

Willis jerked his head at the watch and said: "Something you have to know about our Marion. She says it's immoral to take presents from someone she can't stand the sight of."

"Oh?"

Tabor looked at her and she explained laconically: "From my husband. He went upcountry this morning, and it's my birthday, and when I woke up this was on the dressing table with one of those affectionate cards... Just wanted to show it to Willis, and then I'm giving it right back to him."

He would have been embarrassed, but he saw her smile and began to laugh with her, and when he looked at Markos' cheroot he took out a cigar and waved it and said: "Anybody mind? Ma'am? I mean, Mrs. Cassel?"

"Marion."

"Okay, Marion."

The thin Sudanese waiter, neat and smart in his long white gown and green cummerbund, brought a bottle of ozou and poured a little in their glasses and then added water, and when it turned cloudy, Tabor raised his glass and said, looking at the two Greeks, "Your country gave us civilization, but they also gave us ozou and they should have known better."

He held his drink and waited for the others, looking at Marion and thinking about the cool, composed face and the steady blue eyes that belied the slur—or was it only fancy?—that he detected in her speech. *A beautiful woman, he thought, poised and outgoing but yet withdrawn, infinitely removed from the commonplace and therefore, in spite of the laughter, alone... And the laughter? Does she wish she could join the rest of the world that is really not part of her? Is that it?* He began to think of his wife, and while he thought of her Marion looked away.

Tabor smelled the sweet aniseed scent of the ozou and sighed, and when Marion raised her glass he fancied he saw a slight unsteadiness there again, and he thought for a while about her husband, about the Cassel who used to work for Willis, and knew she was much too good for him.

For a moment their eyes met and held, and she said: "Have you been here long?" She did not call him by name, and it seemed that there was a touch of intimacy there, as though she had known him too long to bother with formalities.

It surprised him, and he said easily: "Three months, a little over."

"I heard about the crocodile hunt." She looked at Willis quickly and laughed and said: "Not the best place for a swim, the Rufiji, is it?"

"I found that out."

"And how long will you stay here?"

He shrugged. "I'm a free man, no plans..."

"I'm trying to persuade him," Willis said, "to make his home here."

Tabor wanted to ask her about her husband, but he looked at Marion and kept quiet, thinking about the skill with which she hid the loneliness, thrusting the display of it away from her as unworthy, knowing that in spite of the joking there was always sympathy for a woman in her position, knowing this and desperately refusing the sympathy. He did not know what it was that had broken the Willis-Cassel arrangement; whatever it was, it did not seem to worry Marion. A bright young man, he thought, who had everything a man could want and did not know how to make use of it. A young man with good looks and easy manners and a careless talent for the hunt...and an attractive wife who had learned to hate him.

And he knew, too, that a woman with a weakling for a husband is on her own, groping, looking for her own roots; he fancied he could see a repressed sadness there, and as he studied her face, admiring the smooth complexion and wondering where the thin lines of sadness came from, he suddenly realized she was watching him too.

He came back to earth with a grimace, and said: "Sorry, was I staring? I've always been susceptible to the mischief a good-looking woman can cause." Smiling, he said: "My only weakness, but I've spent half my life fighting it."

"Fighting it?" She was mocking him gently. "Or running from it?"

"I suppose it comes to the same thing, doesn't it?"

He could sense the effort she was making to hold onto her sobriety, and she said, as if reading his thoughts: "But the beauty is only gin deep."

She poured herself another drink, and Willis said, as though worrying about it for the first time now that someone else had seen it too: "Let's make this the last, shall we?"

"All right." She looked at Tabor and smiled. "Willis is the best friend a man can have, Mr. Tabor, and for a woman... He's my watchdog, a thin, wiry, very determined watchdog, and I love him." She swallowed her drink and turned the glass upside down on the tablecloth and said, "There, you see what a good girl I am? And tonight, I will sleep alone, the Virgin Marion in person." Her eyes did not leave Tabor's face, and she said: "It's going to be a rare night, no one to put me to sleep."

She paused and said: "Are you married, Mr. Tabor?"

"I was. She left me."

"You're a lucky man, do you know that?"

"Maybe I got what I deserved, I don't know."

"Marriage...it's just a way to pay off a debt. And if there's no debt to be paid, then you've made a bad bargain. Is that why you married, Mr. Tabor?"

"No. She was just... a beautiful woman I thought I was in love with, that's all."

"And could she lean on you, as a woman wants to lean on someone? I suppose she could."

"Maybe. I thought so."

"Yes, I suppose she could. I've probably cornered the unreliable

27

husband market myself. Tonight, he's up at Lake Nyanza, and if I know my wretched husband half as well as the rest of the world...he's fast asleep, dead drunk, in some little African wench's bed."

She toyed with the upturned glass for a while, frowning, and Tabor looked away.

Marion Cassel had never quite found what she was looking for. Nor, indeed, was she truly aware of what it was that so dexterously eluded her; she was too complex a woman to give it the simple name of happiness.

She had come out to the Protectorate ten years ago, as a girl of sixteen, to help her father photograph big game in the Nairobi National Park.

Her father was a slight, placid man, mild-tempered and tolerant, who had long since given up trying to control his daughter's sudden bursts of irresponsibility; ever since, in fact, his wife had died and left him with the impossible task of bringing up a fourteen-year-old tomboy whom he deeply loved and did not fully understand.

There had been some trouble at the school, the kind of trouble that caused him unpleasant pangs of guilt because, he thought, if he had sent her to his sister's place as everyone had told him to do she would at least have prepared herself more effectively for the fundamental problems that surround a growing, beautiful girl; and would have understood, perhaps, the answers to at least some of them.

At sixteen, Marion already had the assurance of a grown woman, and there was sometimes a cool placidity in her eyes, a motionlessness to the muscles of her face, that disturbed him deeply; sometimes it seemed as though nothing that went on around her could affect her in the slightest.

She sat there in the Headmistress's office, that miserable day, detached and calm, while the tight-lipped Miss Proctor had said, her face suffused:

"Today, Mr. Davier. I want her out of the school today. We have no room for her anymore. I am sorry to insist, but..."

Marion had watched her father as he looked at the worn threads of the Axminster carpet and said hesitantly: "I don't think she's ever...done...that sort of thing...before... Was it the first time?"

Miss Proctor said coldly, "I doubt it very much. And I do not suppose that it will be the last. It will, however, be the last time *here*."

She had felt nothing about it really, certainly not guilt or shame; though there was a certain sorrow for her father.

His magazine had wanted him to go to Africa, and when Marion had insisted he take her with him, he was too upset to refuse.

And ten days later, the Daviers left for Mombasa.

Right from the beginning, it was not a very successful safari.

Davier had tried to save some of the firm's money by hiring a white hunter who had no license to operate, a man the Association hadn't even heard of. They went off together, all three of them, up to the Northern Province when the elephants were trekking south for water, heading for the swamps on the Ethiopian border.

The white hunter, whose name was Cassel, was a handsome young man, sunburned to a deep brown that hid the premature red veins on his dissipated face, but he was a good shot and he knew his elephants; when he was sober, at least, which was most of the time.

Moving in absolute silence, he would take Davier up to within a few yards of a browsing herd, standing there patiently with his Magnum ready, pointing silently to the best specimens, while Marion, her face burned red and her nose peeling, stood by and watched, half-scared at first and then getting bolder as the weeks went by, learning to stand dead still in the shade of an upwind bush, not moving a muscle, her heart beating fast, listening to the trumpeting in the hot dry air.

Then, on the fifth week out, when it was very early in the morning, they had found a huge bull wandering about by himself, moving slowly, painfully, lethargically, his immense head drooping; his tusks were enormous.

It was Marion who had spotted him first. She had gone down to wash in a pool where the hippos splashed in the mud, just after daybreak and before anyone else was up, because on two occasions before she had seen Cassel watching her surreptitiously while she bathed, hiding himself behind a clump of banana palms; it had not annoyed her, she was proud of her body, but the night before he had been abominably drunk, and there was some reflex in her that, quite innocently, wanted to pay him back for his discourtesy.

And there, by the other side of the pool, was the biggest bull elephant they had yet come across, a huge, lonely, scarred and muddy monster that fascinated her.

Half clothed, she ran back to the camp and woke her father, and when Cassel came out of his tent there was a bottle of whiskey in his hand, although it was only six o'clock, and she knew from the red of his eyes that he had been up all night, drinking alone. It startled her.

Her father went back into his tent to get his cameras, and she said to Cassel curiously: "There can't be much fun in sitting up all night, with just a bottle for company."

He shrugged. "I'd like better company. But the old man keeps an eye on you, doesn't he?"

He was twenty-two years old, long-legged and easy-moving, like an animal, but he did not like the loneliness of his chosen career, and when the sun had gone down he would look around and mutter angrily, "You never saw anything so beautiful in your life, not in the daytime. But at night... Jesus, what the hell is there to do?" The nights were too long for him, and the signs of a premature spoiling were there on his face for the world to see.

But, watching him now, she felt a thrill go through her, a thrill that was associated, not with his fine and delicate features, but with the vicarious essence of a romantic outdoors, of a bush that was a long way from Miss Proctor's, of a man against the elements and of the controlled savagery that has to be in every man who lives, or tries to live, by his rifle.

Cassel turned away sharply and yelled for the head-boy to bring water. When it came he sloshed some over his touseled head and took his Magnum and said briefly, "Let's get after him."

The elephant had gone when they reached the pool, but an hour later they caught up with him, and they stood in the shade of a great anthill five hundred yards away and watched for a while.

Marion silently handed her father the big Graphic he liked for close shots.

Davier said: "Can we get ahead of him? Or turn him around for a head-on shot?"

Cassel nodded. "Only...he's a bad bastard by the looks of him. We'll have to be careful."

"How can you tell?"

"Look at the way he moves. He's dying. Poisoned arrow, probably. If we stuck on his tail long enough..."

Marion saw her father look at Cassel in surprise.

Cassel said, "We can't shoot him without a hunting license, but if we stay with him till he drops dead... That ivory would buy a lot of whiskey."

"I'd rather get a few good shots, head on."

"All right. I'll turn him around for you. Better stand quite still, and don't let him see you."

"How close can we get?"

Cassel grinned at them. "Depends how fast you can run."

"Fifty feet? And I'd like to get him with his ears out."

"You don't want much, do you? They put their ears out, that's the time to start looking for another piece of territory to hang around in."

"A bull that size somehow *ought* to be angry. And he ought to look it."

"Don't worry. If he smells you he'll be angry enough."

Marion was checking the light meter, looking at the sun and saying: "Five point six, but I don't believe it."

"Give it a shade less," her father said. "Just a touch, it's deceptive with all this red sand."

The air was as bracing as cold champagne, clear and sharp and clean.

As Cassel began to move around to the west, Marion whispered, "Shall I take the Leica?"

Her father shook his head, smiling at her enthusiasm. "Not this time. It might be dangerous."

He pointed at a pile of yellow boulders that stood like giant petrified droppings from another age, a cluster of limestone shapes in the empty middle of a hot, eroded plain where the only color was in the soft gray-green of the camel scrub.

"Up on the top. Over there."

31

He was setting the lens of the Graphic and pulling up the finder. She tossed her long hair back from her face and said: "It would be a nice long-shot."

"All right then. But right at the top. I don't want him reaching up there after you."

She looked at the great slow bulk of the retreating elephant, lumbering painfully, heavily, along, and her eyes were sad. She said: "He wouldn't hurt me. Not him."

"Go on, get over there, and do as your father tells you."

When she had gone, he watched her scrambling up the steep yellow bluff, marveling at the agility of her young, supple body, smiling when he thought of the sunburn and the way her hair was already bleaching out in the sun, thinking he had never before seen her so happy, and then he settled down to wait, crouching in the long shadow of the anthill and watching the elephant; looking for Cassel, too, but there was no sign of him.

And then he heard a shrill call like a drunken song, and he knew that Cassel was out there somewhere far away, beginning to turn the animal around and head him into the sun.

It was only eight o'clock in the morning and the shadows were still long over the sand, but he was thirsty and wished they had not come so far from the camp where the servants were. He wanted a cup of tea, and wished he'd brought the thermos bottle along. Waiting, he slipped the hood over the lens of his camera, pointed it towards the yellow rocks where Marion was, and took her picture, then slipped off the hood and reset the aperture.

The shrill calls came again, and as he watched, he saw the elephant, waving its trunk in the air and scenting, six hundred yards away and more now; and then it turned and began to move slowly back, away from the unseen danger that was Cassel. It lumbered heavily, its great head moving from side to side. The sun was white on its tusks.

He could see Cassel now, far in the distance behind the gray bulk, his gun held loosely in his hand, moving out into the open to change his position. He checked the camera again and waited. When he looked back towards Marion, he saw that she was standing up on the pinnacle of her rock, and he signaled to her to squat down, squinting against the sun as he did so. Obediently, she dropped to her haunches, and he looked again at the elephant, still moving steadily towards him.

When it was a hundred yards away, he steadied himself with his feet wide-spaced and took his first picture, and then took another, and then another, wondering at the size of the image in the view finder. He checked the focus quickly and moved the lens forward a touch, hearing the sound of the shutter, immense in the heavy silence, and then the elephant stopped and seemed to look straight at him. Its giant ears began to move ponderously, almost in slow motion, and he felt his heartbeat quicken, and he thought: *He's seen me...*

The huge head was back now, and there was no sickness on the animal anymore, but only a sudden and frightening assumption of angry power. It began to move towards him, stepping up its pace and beginning to charge; and he stepped out from his cover to get a better shot, forcing himself to hold the camera still, rewinding the film without taking his eyes off the target, watching it with a cool deliberation he did not know he possessed. The earth shook under his feet.

The silence was acute, and he half-expected Cassel to shout a warning to him to move away, and then, the wire frame of the finder was filled with the looming black bulk and he pressed the release and dived to one side as the elephant went past him, trumpeting angrily now, the earth rumbling under the weight of it.

He rolled over on his back as he fell, thinking only of the fine sand and the delicate glass of the lens, and then the elephant was pounding savagely at the anthill; he watched it fly apart under the heavy blows of the trunk and thought with alarm of the other camera there, glad that Marion had taken the Leica with her. In triumph, he clicked the shutter twice.

Somewhere, not far away, he heard Cassel's voice, filled with sudden alarm. "Keep still, don't move, don't make a sound..." The voice was a shout that was colored with sudden fear, and the fear came to him, too, a cold mist of fear that brought sweat to the palms of his hands. A thorn was buried deep in his back where he had fallen, and there were gray spikes of an unnamed shrub feeling for his face, but he kept still, not daring to turn his head, looking sideways at the towering bulk of the elephant, no more than ten paces away now, still thrashing savagely at the anthill, pounding its enormous front feet into the soil with a resurgence of petulant strength. The trunk went up again, and a mighty sound came from it that made his blood turn cold, and the great body swung around so that the tusks, huge-curved and framed against the sky, lost their whiteness and took on a tinge of red-gray high above him.

A foot that seemed more than a yard across pounded deep into the earth beside him, leaving an imprint that was six inches deep, and he knew that the elephant had left his ant-hill and found the true cause of his anger and was moving in to attack. He waited in alarm for the sound of Cassel's gun that must, he knew, come now, and he thought in desperation: *What's he doing? Why isn't he shooting? This is what he's there for...*

He rolled over quickly, in panic now, and leaped to his feet with an unaccustomed agility, racing for the rocks that were more than a hundred yards away. He heard a shot ring out and the relief flooded over him, and there was another shot and then another; but over it all was the pounding sound of an express train behind him, the earth quivering with the weight of it, and his relief went quickly away as he heard Marion begin to scream. The thoughts came to him wildly: *Three shots, he can't have missed, he can't, they never do*...and he looked over his shoulder in fear and almost squealed when he saw how close the huge bulk was. All he could hear now was Marion's screaming.

He saw her, standing up on the rocks high above, quite clearly, her hands to her face and her mouth open.

The piercing scream was the last sound he heard as the huge, searching trunk took him at the waist and effortlessly crushed the life from him, not deliberately but with the unconscious strength of the anger that was there.

Then his broken body hurtled into the side of the rock, to be picked up and flung again and again at the stones, until all that was left was a scattered pulp on which the elephant slowly, methodically, began to pound its giant feet.

Then the elephant sank to its haunches, felt at the air for a moment with its trunk, and toppled over onto its side as Cassel, white as a ghost, came running up, still firing and pumping his Magnum.

Marion, numbed with shock, half-fell, half-slid from her perch, and when she reached the ground it was to land on the hard, still quivering flesh of the dead elephant that felt like a trembling volcanic rock beneath her, still hot with the ancient, angry fires.

For a moment she looked about her, not understanding, not conscious of her own consciousness, and then when she saw the red marks on the sand that were all that was left of her father, she moaned faintly and fell to the ground.

Cassel stood beside her, open mouthed, shaking the disbelief from his mind, stuttering his fear and saying drunkenly: "I hit him...four times, I hit him, I know I did."

She could only shake her head, and the blankness in her eyes frightened him badly. She did not speak, or look at him, or cry, until they had slowly found their way back to the camp where the stolid Nandi servants were, and there she lay on her canvas cot for the rest of the day, staring up at the gray shadows on the big thorn tree that was their marker.

In the morning, Cassel took her back to Nairobi. And six months later, he married her.

CHAPTER 3

They met again, Marion and Tabor, three months after that night in the Greek restaurant, and five hundred miles away; it was a coincidence of time and place of the kind that prompts the superstitious to believe in the calculated nature of chance.

Over the vast waters of Lake Victoria, there was not a ripple or a sound to ruffle the infinite tranquility; the water was as motionless as the rest of the world around it, and there was silence in the thick vegetation at the water's edge where, he knew, the elephants he was tracking had gone, though he could not hear them.

Tabor was on his own, out after the last elephant on his license, and for two days he had followed the spoor, and now he was close among the herd, creeping out carefully along a narrow spit of land that jutted out into the lake like the tongue of an animal.

Willis, his tutor, had looked at him shrewdly and had said: "Yes, you're capable enough on your own, if that's what you really want. Is it so important to you?"

"You've been holding my hand for six months now."

"But I'll see you again before you leave?"

"Leave? I'm not going anywhere."

Surprised, Willis had said: "I'm glad to hear it, we need men like you out here."

"Men like me?" Tabor snorted. "You figure you really know what that means?" He said morosely: "Something I've got to get out of my system, and I don't even know what it is, not anymore."

"But whatever it is, you can take it out on the animals, is that it?"

"You're a hell of a man to argue the morals of hunting." Willis laughed and said: "All right, if there's anything I can do to help..."

"Just let me know where you'll be when I get back"

"Porters? Gunbearers?"

"I'm going alone."

The sun was directly overhead here, at midday, beating down fiercely onto the red sandstone, and the green of the trees at the edge of the water was so bright it was almost painful to look at. The acacia trees had enriched themselves on the swampy sludge of the banks, and their foliage was lush and brilliant, heavy with the weight of the water in the leaves. The trunks of the great baobabs were fifteen feet across and more, and the air was heavy with the ripe scent of juniper.

He could see the great bull, out there at the tip of the spit, and he passed quietly among the browsing females of the herd, close to them, moving cautiously and ready to run, and when he was a hundred yards away he could clearly see the tiny arrow that was hanging from the elephant's belly, no more than eighteen inches long but tipped, he knew, with poison. This then, was the reason for the roguery...

In the village where he had left his truck, the Tribal Elders had told him: "All our crops, *Bwana*, trampled and uprooted, and where shall we find food for the winter?" Four of the mud-and-wattle houses on the edge of the village had been savagely smashed, and a weeping woman had been searching hopelessly in the ruins for the remnants of her cooking vessels while the men had stolidly watched her, unfeeling for her sorrow because, after all, she was only a woman. The big bull, they had told him, had gone to rejoin the herd down at the water's edge a day's march away to the south, and for two nights he had slept close by the huge mounds of excreta that told him the elephant was nearby, wrapping himself in a blanket against the bitter cold of the night and wishing, sometimes, that he had brought a servant with him as all the other hunters did.

And now the great herd was close by, surrounding him, the

quietly browsing females reaching up into the treetops with their quaquaversal trunks and searching out the tender shoots. There was so much peace on them that he felt a pang of sorrow for what he had to do, and he stood by a clump of Strychnos trees and waited till the bull should turn to face him. As he watched, he heard a low whistle and looked around in surprise to see Marion there, watching him, silent. half-smiling, crouched in the shadows of a lump of granite that jutted preposterously out of the earth...

He raised his eyebrows and put a finger to his lips and she nodded and came quickly over to him, moving as silently as he himself did, and they shook hands without a word and looked at the bull together for a little while.

Then she put her mouth close to his ear and whispered: "I've been watching both of you for the last half hour. I saw you coming down the spit. You know the rest of the herd has moved in behind us? It'll be hard to get back."

In the dense scrub, they were invisible, but he could hear them champing, tearing at the branches. He took her hand and led her gently away, downwind a little, and then, when it was safe to talk quietly, he grinned at her and whispered: "I didn't think the day could be improved, but... What the hell are you doing up here?"

She held up the Leica for him to see.

"For the *Geographical Magazine*, if they turn out well enough. I got some fine shots of the herd, and I was trying to get close to the bull. He's been wounded." She looked at his gun and said: "Do you have to kill him?"

He nodded. "That's what I came here for. He's been beating up the villages."

"I know."

"And still it makes you sad."

"I have better reason not to feel sorry for elephants."

Willis had told him about her father, and he kept silent.

She said: "All the same, it seems a pity. He's full of arrows, did you see them?"

"I saw one. In the belly."

"The pygmies. They creep underneath them and shoot upwards. But he doesn't think he's dying or he wouldn't have rejoined the herd."

"Yes, I know." Tabor looked at her in sudden surprise and said: "Where did you leave your truck? I didn't hear it."

She gestured. "Back there. Five miles or more back there. And yours?"

"In Felusa. I followed the spoor on foot." He grimaced. "Two days and nights."

"And no boys?" She was still smiling at him. "That's no way to hunt."

"Oh, I don't know... Seems to me you people make too much fuss about it. Servants, porters, gunbearers, drivers, water boys, that's not a safari, that's an expedition."

"A loner."

It came as a sudden shock to him. He said slowly: "That's what my wife used to call me. She didn't approve. But is it so wrong to want to be... out here, in the middle of nowhere, with nothing but the animals and...and God for company?"

"The animals and God...that's a fancy combination." Mocking him, she said: "And if you weren't shooting God's animals, I still wouldn't believe you'd altogether rejected the company of men. And of women."

"No, not really." He stared at the bull elephant and said soberly: "You know, just a couple of months back I'd have been after him for the size of his tusks alone. The splendid specimen that has to be killed just because he is splendid."

"And now?"

"Now I'm not sure anymore. For a while there it seemed that using a gun was all I was good for."

"And now that you've found your *metier*, you don't like it anymore."

"I'm beginning to feel sorry for anything I have to kill, let's put it like that." He laughed quickly and said: "Just beginning to, that's all."

"That's a hell of a conclusion for a hunter to come to, isn't it? But they all do, in time, they just get sick on a surfeit of blood, sooner or later. All except my husband, that is... If you want a man who really takes pleasure in killing... It's the only way he can prove what a

39

hell of a man he is." She turned to him and touched his hand and said: "I'm glad for the beginning."

He held her look for a long time. He said at last: "And that poor old bull has still got to be shot. If you'd seen the damage he's done..."

He stood up and looked around at the long spit of land.

The bull was at the extreme tip, close to the water, his great head drooping so that the long tusks raked the ground. Tabor turned and looked back towards the base of the isthmus, searching for the rest of the herd; he could see nothing, and he said, worrying about it for her sake: "If we stampede them, I suppose they'll head for the land..."

She followed his look and nodded. "Sure to."

But they were wrong. The first shot struck the rogue in the center of the depression of the forehead, and the bullet, shattering, blew out the brain; the elephant sank slowly to its knees, swayed for a moment, and then rolled over on its side, and Marion just had time to say: "A good shot, a merciful shot..." and then the herd was coming at them, charging not towards the land but towards the tip of the isthmus where they stood, trumpeting their fear.

Tabor grabbed at her and yelled: "Run...this way...!"

He dragged her to the water's edge, and then they were up to their waists in mud, splashing back towards the mainland as the herd thundered past them.

She fell, and he dragged her to her feet, gasping for breath, and pulled her along with him, forcing his way into the slime just as he had done that day with Willis down in the swamps of the Rufiji. She was reaching under the water for her camera and he shouted: "Leave it, I'll buy you a new one!" and she staggered against him and pointed and he raised his gun calmly and fired at a crocodile that was making steadily towards them, watching with satisfaction the sudden angry flurry that told him he had hit it.

She said: "The hell with the camera, I've lost some good shots."

They staggered together towards the shore, and when they reached it and stumbled up onto the bank, she looked at the mud all over her and said: "God, what a bloody mess!"

She held her arms out from her sides and looked at herself, tall and slim and lithe, with the black mud clinging to her and dripping down her breast, and he began to laugh at her, and she went panting to a path of green turf and threw herself down on it on her back, stretching out her legs and her arms in the hot sun and looking up at him as he laughed, and suddenly she was quite serious and all his laughter was gone too.

He looked at her soberly and then knelt down beside her and touched her shoulder and said: "Are you all right, Marion? Are you all right?"

She did not answer. Instead, she began to slide her fingers over her body, pulling away the black sludge that clung to her, knowing that he was watching her and knowing that the excitement was rising in him. He did not move, but stayed there on his knees, close by her, his hands hanging loosely down at his sides, curved inwards as though he were waiting to seize her.

She shook the shirt loose from her body and said: "I could take these clothes off and wash them...or just let them dry and shake the mud off."

He still did not move, and there was an expression on his face that she could not fully understand, and she looked up at him and said mildly, making a joke of it: "You could help by scraping some of this mud off me."

He leaned towards her then, and began to scoop the slime off her, scraping the flat of his hand along her flank and flicking the mud off, then scraping away at her long calves and her thighs and her stomach. She closed her eyes and let his hands move over her, and when she opened them again to look at him, wondering, she saw that he was trembling a little, hesitating, not sure of himself. She undid the buttons of her shirt and shook the cloth, pulling it stickily away from her breast, and when he stopped moving his hands and looked at her she said: "You need a hell of a lot of prompting, don't you?"

He began to choose his words carefully, but before he could speak she reached down and took his hand and laid it on her breast and said: "For God's sake, don't you know when a woman's asking you to make love?"

He let his hand stay there for a moment, unmoving, and then he took it away and said gently: "No, Marion, not now."

Surprised, she sat up and stared at him in disbelief. The laughter was there on her face in a brightness of the eyes, no more, and she said incredulously: "I never came across a man who didn't think I was the most beautiful woman he'd ever met. For the moment, of course. Even covered over from head to foot with wet mud."

"It's not that at all."

"Then what is it?" The laughter was going before it could break out, and there was a touch of asperity coming there in its place.

He said slowly, groping for his words: "I've known you...how long, Marion? A couple of months? We met once. Only once."

"What the hell has that got to do with it?"

"You know nothing about me, nothing at all."

"I know you're not a bloody eunuch. Or are you? Is that it?"

The asperity had hardened still more. She began to move, angrily getting to her feet, but he put a hand on her shoulder and stopped her, and he said again: "We met once, Marion, this is only the second time... We know nothing about each other."

She still did not believe him. She took hold of his hand and removed it from her shoulder, letting it drop almost contemptuously, and she stood up, standing with her feet wide apart and her fists on her hips, bedraggled and wild and somehow looking like part of the wet soil of the lake itself. Her clothes still clung to her wetly, and her hair hung down untidily, but he thought that no woman had ever looked more infinitely desirable.

She said again, savagely: "Is that it? Is that what it is?"

He began to smile now, containing her anger, and he put up his hands and held her at the hips, and said: "I'm on my knees in front of you..."

He climbed to his feet, still holding her, and pulled her tight to him, holding her so tightly that the great hands dug deep into her flesh; she could feel the pressure on the hipbone, hurting her, and she looked up at him in surprise and he slid his arms up her back and leaned down and kissed her and said: "I don't want a casual thing, Marion, can you understand that?"

Speaking through her surprise, still angry, she said: "Not like all the others? Is that what you mean?"

"Yes, if you want to put it like that. Not like all the others."

"You're charmingly frank, aren't you?"

"If, and when...it's got to be more than that."

"Well, I'll be damned."

"Does it surprise you that I want...more of you than the others?"

"You sound pretty convinced there *are* others."

"You've never tried to hide your..."

As he fumbled for the word, she said: "Notoriety? No. Why the hell should I?"

"Does it sound like preaching to say I don't like crowds?"

"The bloody nerve. The brash, bloody nerve."

He did not move his arms away from her; it was as though he were trying to force her into a pattern. He said stubbornly: "If lousing this up is the only way I can tell you, that's what I'll do. You're too good to...to waste, and that's what it would be. A waste. I don't want that."

"I'll be...damned to hell."

She could feel the heat in the hands that gripped her shoulder blades, pressing into her; they were strong, unyielding, rigid even when she began to pull away from him, holding her firmly as though the strength of his own determination were in them, as though only by physical inflexibility could he bring home to her the force of his own resolve.

He said, smiling still: "Now go and get cleaned up, you look like the witch of Endor."

The pressure of the hands was suddenly gone, and she said: "For God's sake, I ought to belt you one across the face."

She left him then, and went behind a rock and took off her shirt and trousers and rinsed them out in the clear water of a tiny inlet where the white pebbles caught the sun, and spread them out in the hot sun to dry, and he sat under the shade of a clump of hazel saplings and waited for her, smoking, wondering, thinking about her and knowing that his insistence had brought them suddenly, immeasurably closer together.

And, when she came to join him at last, with her clothes creased but clean, and her face bright and shining and her hair swirled around on top of her head and pinned there, they went off together to find the trucks, holding hands like shy lovers.

Once or twice she looked up at him as he walked beside her,

43

searching her own mind for anger or for affection and finding neither, finding instead only a bewilderment and a strange uneasiness.

When they came to her truck, she drove him back to Felusa, and when they parted, he took her hand and said: "We'll meet again soon?"

"Soon."

He watched her drive away, and then went to tell the Elders about the bull elephant, to send out the boys with the meat knives, and when they asked him about the tusks, he said briefly: "Keep them, sell them, do what you like with them." He wondered how soon he would see her again.

But the next time he met her, nearly two weeks later, it was at a party on one of the ships in the harbor, where she was dancing with a young French tourist, leaning against him drunkenly, letting him paw at her, swaying on her feet and not caring. When she saw him, she startled, and looked at him resentfully; and in a little while she went outside onto the deck with her Frenchman and leaned on the rail looking down into the deep waters of the inlet.

He saw them once through the long windows of the lounge, locked tight in each other's arms, and as he looked they turned away together and went down the companionway to where the cabins were.

CHAPTER 4

Throughout the Territories, the rumblings of discontent could be heard. The old days were passing, and no one was ready for the new. The new morality was an alien concept, only faintly noticed and not really understood, because what the rest of the world was doing had never really mattered very much in Africa.

The sounds of agitation that came from the rest of the world were a source of amusement more than anything else, because the idea that it can't happen here, which had passed over other continents and left its disproof behind it, was still firmly entrenched; the whites were secure in their superiority, the blacks had always accepted their tertiary status, and the Indians in the middle...well, no one really bothered very much about the Indians; they had long ago taken complete economic control through their aptitude for hard work and perseverance. The Asians were the merchants, almost exclusively, and no one grudged them the position with which they seemed to be adequately content.

The division of society here was arbitrary and peculiar, and could exist, perhaps, nowhere else in the world. All white men, even if they came from America, were officially classed as *Europeans*; all brown men, even if they had been born in Africa, were *Asians*; and all the others, the blacks, were *Africans*. This was the official and the accepted nomenclature, and the rigid differentiation, dictated by a nonelected if benevolent Government and generally approved by society itself, was firmly entrenched in spite of its attendant anomalies.

The fourth-generation settler's son who had never left the Usumbura Highlands was still a European, whether he liked it or not; the Somalis, living in their dreary deserts for more than eight hundred years were officially Asians (by long and involved litigation they had made it so themselves); and the American Negro off the ship in the harbor was an African the moment he stepped ashore, because his skin was black and that was the end of it.

The three societies kept to themselves, in their own areas, their own clubs, their own tight little circles, each unconcerned with the others until the murmurings from abroad began to be heard.

The times were changing. Only the white man could make the radios, the roads, the telegraphs, and the railways that brought the alien news in, and this monopolistic security could never be endangered as long as the white man held the reins. But when the white man himself began to question his own authority—sometimes through knowledge and sometimes through ignorance—the whole structure began to fall apart. At both extremes of the social order the changes were to be violent and definitive; but in the center of the order, the Asians stood hesitant, unsure, and deeply worried.

The days and the weeks and the months slipped by, casually, as though tomorrow were as assured as today, as though the future were as deeply rooted by custom as the past.

But it was not to be so. The headlines in the local press touched on the affairs of other parts of the continent at first with something like scorn, then with astonishment, and finally with a good deal of alarm.

And within the space of a few years, the rumblings finally grew in a crescendo that could no longer be ignored.

The heat, that night, had been intolerable.

All day long the clouds had hung so close to the earth that it seemed the spire of the old-fashioned church on the main street would pierce them and release the laden rain; but the rain would not come, and you could almost pray that the heat would swell to breaking point and bring the rain and the relief pouring down from the heavens in a torrent that would flood the streets, ankle deep, in less than five minutes.

Sometimes Babajee wished he had bought one of the big new houses down on the beach at Oyster Bay, but his native wisdom had prevailed, and when his friends would say: "But Baba, with your money, a house at Oyster Bay, isn't it?" he would answer with remarkably even humor: "No, my friend, as long as there is one Englishman who wishes, even if he doesn't say it, that the Asians would stay out of Oyster Bay, I will keep to my poor old house here." He would add craftily: "Nearly all my customers are English, and it is easier to charge them a little bit extra for the implied indignities they make me suffer, than to have them ask what is that bloody Babajee doing with a house at Oyster Bay... Besides, with today's prices... You think I could build a house like this one for less than twenty thousand pounds? No, my friend, I will wait."

Nobody would ask him what he was waiting for; everyone knew, and it would always make them silent, thoughtful, wondering.

They could read the local papers, and the *Telegraph* and the *Guardian* flown out from London, and they knew that sooner or later there would be very few Englishmen left at Oyster Bay or anywhere else. But who would replace them?... There, they were not so sure. Only Babajee was sure. He would say: "When the English have gone, the Africans will still need a ruling class, isn't it? You think they can rule themselves? Of course not! You will see, my friend. Wait, and you will see."

But that was before the hatred of the Asians became so much stronger than the Africans' need of them. It was before the burnings of the Asian stores and the Asian sisal sheds, and the Asian warehouses...

Now, the tide had begun to show more clearly which way it would run. Some of the Indians were already preparing to leave, but Babajee would say, a little uneasily: "I cannot believe that the English will abandon us completely. They are our friends." And when he was asked, a little peremptorily, what the English were expected to do if they themselves were to be unceremoniously kicked out of the country, he would raise his hands and protest: "But it was the same in India. We invited them to leave, and less than a year later we were inviting them all back again. The African, too, will learn that he cannot manage without them..."

And so, for the time being, there was a show of friendliness, a careful hiding of the old distrusts and a careful shielding of them so that they could never grow into real hatred; so that they could never get beyond the bounds of a tolerant acceptance; and in the Asian society, acceptance was becoming important word.

That night, in the shadows under the big mimosa tree that stood by the wrought-iron gate where the name *Ramatool Upaboy Babajee* had been painted in English rather than in Gujerati, there was not a breeze to stir the delicate tracery of the leaves.

All day long the closed shutters had kept the heat of the blasting sun away from the rooms, but with nightfall the heat had become even more intense, even more moist, so that the guests mopped at the sweat on the backs of their necks and wished they could lie on the beaches in bathing costumes instead of sitting stiffly around on the gilt-and-scarlet chairs that lined the big drawing room in meticulous precision around the whitewashed walls.

Marion's latest friend, Gerald Scott, was there that night, as cold and alert and as smoothly confident as ever. He stood in the doorway that led to the small garden, letting the scent of the frangipani smother him, feeling the sensuous delight in it, waiting for the Cassels. He looked back into the room and saw the pretty little Punjabi girl, Petna, sitting shyly on one of the brocaded chairs and trying to attract, by her very immobility, the attention of that lout Bradley who was pouring himself a glass of pale pink punch.

Bradley was the District Officer from somewhere upcountry, a thin, nervous young man with peering eyes and the immature zeal of a reformer. He was despised by the settlers because he had brought with him, from London, the new socialist concept of a world full of equals. He believed deeply in those concepts, and he could not understand why a man should be different because of his pigmentation. The Europeans distrusted him, and the Africans hated him; and like all median thinkers, he had found his niche in the middle. He was talking to Gregory, one of the Greeks who owned an obscure hotel on the other side of the harbor channel.

The orchestra was playing a German waltz, a little off key, and Gerald Scott sighed and went into the garden, sipping his whiskey and waiting.

And then the big Bedford station wagon that Marion used drew up, and he walked to the gate and held it open for her. She brushed by him without a word, but she was aware of the look in his eyes, and then Cassel was there too, slapping him on the back and saying heartily: "Gerald, old boy, what sort of drinks have they got here?"

Gerald gestured with his glass. "If you're wise, you'll keep away from that abominable punch. But there's plenty of Scotch."

"Thank God and Mr. bloody Babajee." Cassel peered towards the open door, looked over the crowd, and said thickly: "The whole bloody Colony... What's he trying to prove?"

"All very simple," Gerald said. "We have to treat them now as if they were our equals. Though not, of course, as if *we* were *theirs*. And Babajee is very anxious to show his appreciation."

Cassel said: "That'll take a hell of a lot of whiskey."

"And there's a hell of a lot there."

Cassel staggered away. Gerald looked after him with distaste and the thought of those stubby hunter's hands probing at Marion's body sickened him.

Cassel paused at the door and looked back and said, as an afterthought, attaching no importance to it: "Marion wanted to know if you'd be here. I said, sure, you knew she was coming."

The bright lights of the room behind him shaded his face, and then he turned back again and went inside.

Gerald sipped his drink and said aloud, quite quietly: "One day, you bastard, you'll get your comeuppance."

He started at a sound beside him, and Petna was there. He was so surprised he looked back into the room to make sure she had left her seat, and said, smiling: "If you heard that, forget it. How are you, Petna?"

She nodded at him, her skin shining, then showed her teeth in a quick smile. She said: "Mr. Cassel's all right, really. He just drinks a little too much."

"Sure he is. A nice fellow. What are you drinking?"

"Punch. It's delicious, shall I get you some?"

He shook his head and said gravely: "No, I'd better stick to whiskey."

She said: "Have you seen the moonflower?"

"No, I don't think I have."

"Then let me show you."

She took his arm impulsively and he went with her to a corner of the garden by the hedge. There was a great white single blossom there, palely reflecting the moon, its curved petals tinged with lavender.

She touched it delicately with the tips of her fingers, and she said: "Once every seven years... The last time it bloomed I was a child."

"And now, Petna?"

"Now I am a woman. Soon, I am going to be married."

"And that's what you wanted to talk to me about." It was a flat statement rather than a question.

She hesitated, and then said very quietly: "I wanted to...to get your opinion."

"Mine only?"

"You know what I mean."

"Don't expect me to speak for the others. There are too many of them."

"But if you...accept it...then most of the others will."

He was surprised. "A radical? Is that what you take me for?"

"No, of course not. But...tonight, my father will announce our engagement, and...to tell the truth, it frightens me a little. It frightens him, too."

Gerald shrugged. "Why should it frighten either of you? He's old enough to tell you what to do. And you're old enough to do as you're told."

She did not know there was venom in his voice; venom was very foreign to her.

He laughed quickly and said: "In all the years I've been here...this is the first interracial marriage I've heard of. Except for the Greeks, of course, and they don't really count, do they?"

She blinked her eyes at him, and he found it suddenly hard to be cruel to her. She said, "I don't see why not..."

"You're too young, Petna, too young to see anything."

"But..."

"Skip it. Just a piece of private malice."

She shook her head at him and he took pleasure in watching the swirl of the long hair.

Raising his glass he said: "I hope you'll be very happy."

"But you don't think we will be?"

He said brutally: "I know damn well you won't be. But not for the reasons you expect me to put forward." He could feel the alarm that was on her. He moved closer to her and put a hand on her shoulder and said gravely: "There aren't many people who know what I know, Petna, and I only know it by chance; and if you tell me I'm wrong I'll believe you and forget all about it." She trembled; he could feel the movement of her skin under his fingers. He lowered his voice and said: "You see, I know about you and Willis."

She was suddenly cold to his touch, and the blood had drained from her face. She looked back over her shoulder in panic, and he said gently: "But not to worry. I don't think anybody else does. And I also know why you're marrying that clot Bradley instead of one of your own people; it's because your father wants the British beside him when the trouble comes, and this is an easy way to do it. Maybe it's a smart move, I don't know."

She said quietly, masking her hurt: "I know that what my father wants me to do is right."

"In spite of Willis?"

"In spite of everything."

Gerald looked at her closely. "You love one man and marry another, just like in the storybooks, and this is supposed to lead you into the twentieth century. Doesn't make sense, does it?"

She said steadily: "Bradley will make me a good husband. He does not think like most of the British."

"You can say that again." Scott swallowed his drink and said, a little thickly: "All right, the times are changing, and it won't be hard for a colored wife to be accepted, not in the circles Bradley moves in. Maybe even your own people will accept it because they respect your father and know that he's trying to move with the times. But, if I know Willis as well as I think I do, he's not going to leave you alone just because you married someone else. I suspect there's a desperation inside him that just won't let him."

She was looking at him strangely. Her eyes were huge and dark and solemn, expectant, waiting for him to make his thoughts clear to her.

He said very gravely: "I'll give you a minute of sobriety, Petna, because you're too nice a woman to get hurt. And then...then the hell with it, you're on your own. My sober advice is, forget this Bradley lout, and make Willis marry you."

For a long time she said nothing. It was as though she were examining minutely all that he was refraining from saying.

She said at last: "Willis won't marry me."

"You can make him."

"No."

"You must know *why* he won't."

"I *think* I do."

"There's a ghost that won't let him. That's all it is, a ghost, but a ghost he can't forget. He wants to make sure he doesn't destroy something he loves, not again, by loving it too much." He said sarcastically: "And he'd be horrified if you told him he was just trying not to get hurt again."

"Another hurt like that would kill any man."

"Marry *him*, Petna. You can still have lots of *chi-chi* kids, if that's the brave new world you want."

"No. I will not hurt him by making him face his hurt."

"You'd rather give yourself to that useless bastard?"

She said stubbornly, brushing aside the crudity: "He is a good man, Bradley. And he loves me."

Gerald looked at his empty glass and said: "This sort of talk, I need another drink."

From inside the house there was a sudden burst of laughter and a tray of glasses crashed to the marble floor.

He said: "That party's getting wild. A good party."

"You haven't answered my question."

He looked at her with a touch of anger and said: "All right, I'll tell you what you want to know. They'll accept you as Bradley's wife, because you are young, and lovely, and too kind to be snubbed. Does that make you happy?"

"Yes, it does."

"But most of us will think it's a waste of a lovely young body. All the men will, at least."

She smiled, a quiet, hesitant young woman feeling her way. "Where we're going...there won't be so much...so much of a problem, perhaps."

"I didn't know you were leaving?" There was regret in his voice, as though she, too, were part of his world.

"My father is moving upcountry for a while, and I will go with him."

"Oh? We'll miss you."

She twisted her glass in her long thin fingers and said slowly: "The Northern Frontier. Bradley is being posted there, and...Baba has bought an old transport company up there, on the desert route, just a few trucks, really, but..." She laughed, and said quickly: "You know my father, he can't resist a good investment."

"Especially when the new District Officer is one of the family. He won't have much competition, will he?"

Not meeting his eye, Petna said: "No...no, I suppose he won't."

"And now I've hurt your feelings. Don't worry, it's just my natural malice. Your father's a good businessman, I won't grudge him his money."

He moved his hand down to her hip, and she slipped quickly aside; and then she took his arm as though in chagrin and said quickly: "But you've frightened me, too."

"About Willis?"

"Yes. Although you said if I denied it you'd believe me."

"And I will."

"Then, I do deny it," she said very clearly. "Willie is a good friend, no more. He has never touched me."

"Of course."

She reached up and kissed him on the lips, very quickly, and he held her narrow waist in his hands and said: "All the same, I wish I were in his place."

"And thank you, Gerald. You're a good friend, too."

He held her for a moment, keeping the pressure of his hands at her waist, and then he said: "Times are changing all right. Only a couple of years ago, if an Indian girl had said that to me...I'd have had her on her back inside five minutes."

She moved away from him with a quick wriggle, and took his hands and said: "The times have not changed. It's only our acceptance of them. I must go back to our guests."

She was gone.

Gerald looked at the moonflower for a while and then wandered into the house to find Marion. For a long time he looked for her in the crowd, and when at last he found her she was in one of the upstairs rooms, lying on the bed and crying her heart out.

Not speaking, he went over and touched her on the shoulder and she looked up at him, dabbed at her eyes, and said roughly: "Let's get back down to the bar, Gerald. I need a drink. A lot of drinks."

"You'd better fix your mascara first."

She nodded and then smiled at him and sighed, and said: "What a bloody fool."

"I'll wait for you downstairs."

Worrying about her, he went back to the bar. Cassel was there, too, pawing at one of the girls who had been hired to dance for them. He looked at Gerald and grinned.

The drum rolled, and the violin screeched painfully, and the dancers took up their positions, smiling, waiting, watching. Their brown eyes were bright, their faces eager. They took their stance, and then began to move, very slowly, around in their circle, crossing their sticks and slapping them brusquely together, and then the reed pipe took up the melody.

Babajee sidled over to Gerald and said confidentially: "A very ancient dance, Mr. Scott, more than three thousand years old. Just as they used to dance it in the time of the Aryan invasions. Even then our civilization was much superior to theirs, and this dance is described in one of the hymns of the Rig-Veda."

Gerald, wondering why he was listening to this, said politely: "Oh, really?"

Babajee peered at trim myopically, wondering how he could break through the barrier of aloof disdain, knowing the desperate urgency of the major step—the step from the middle group, which would disappear, to one of the major groups...and the one that would survive, if only after a period of alarm and disorder. To move *down*, to befriend the hated Africans, or to move *up* and befriend the disdainful whites... To seek acceptance where it could be found...to fool the blacks who were more easily fooled, and more dangerous, or to flatter the English and move their lot with them, this was the question.

He shuttered when he thought of the when he thought of the choice. The anger of the blacks came out in violence, not in black-tie contempt, and sometimes he did not know which was the worse. An angry Englishman would draw on his cigarette and make a bitingly cruel witticism, but an angry African... The *panga* was sharper than the Englishman's contempt. The physical ill, in the course of history, would breed less harm than the equally savage scorn, but it was the present in which the blood was flowing, and history could take care of itself... Or could it?

He said again, smiling desperately: "Three thousand years old, Mr. Scott. And even then, my country's civilization was really quite advanced. In those days, they believed that only pain and pleasure were of consequence, that vice and virtue were nothing more than academic propositions to intrigue the intellect. The striking together of the sticks which the dancers hold, signifies the clash of these two forces; the pleasure in the right hand and the pain in the left."

Gerald was thinking: *If only they wouldn't try so bloody hard!* He said callously: "I bet when you go riding, the horse tries to bite you."

Startled, Babajee said: "I beg your pardon?"

Gerald waved a hand that was meant to indicate the over-immaculate cut of his host's dinner jacket. He said unpleasantly: "I bet even a horse would disapprove of the cut of your clothes."

Cassel came over and slapped Babajee on the back and said loudly: "Dear old boy, with Baba's kind of money you can dress how you bloody well please."

Gerald did not like Cassel, and tonight it showed. He turned away and walked off without a word.

Babajee looked at Cassel and said unhappily: "Such a good man, really, but he can be very cruel when he wants to, wouldn't you say? Really, I paid quite a lot of money for this suit."

Cassel put an arm over his shoulder and said confidentially: "Think nothing of it, old boy. He's got woman trouble." He looked blearily at Babajee and wondered why he seemed to be swaying on his feet, and then he looked around the room and said: "And where the hell's that bloody wife of mine?" His fingers twitched on Babajee's shoulders, and he said: "Trouble with this house, old boy, you've got too many bedrooms. Let a bloody nympho loose in a house like this, not a hope in hell of finding her anywhere."

Babajee considered for a moment (moving from one society into another) and then said carefully: "In ancient India, Mr. Cassel, a woman of extraordinary sexual appetite was considered to be a particularly gratifying gift from the gods. But today, we live in a more *practical* society where the natural passions have become subjugated to the demands of a rather functional expedience; wouldn't you say that, Mr. Cassel?"

Cassel said, startled: "No, by God, I wouldn't say that. But come to think of it, you've got a point there, if only I could understand it."

The sound of the orchestra was coming in, and he heard Babajee saying: "According to the Buddhists, and of course, one cannot really approve of their philosophy, woman is merely one of the carnal delights created by a generous God for the delectation of the supreme being, Man."

He hoped he was finding his way into the tight, restricted circle. But Cassel merely shrugged and said, his eyes a little glazed: "Brother, you'd get along fine with my wife. Come to think of it, she'd probably agree with you. Boys and girls together, black, white, and bloody coffee-colored."

He turned away and went to the bar, and he said to the turbaned Nubian barman: "Fill it up, *brother*."

Babajee stared unhappily after him and went looking for his daughter Petna.

She was with Bradley when he found her, holding onto his arm and smiling at him, looking up at him with wide-eyed assurance which derived from the intimate touch of his body.

He had never seen Bradley look so happy. He smiled and said

gently (he found it hard to speak in anything but gentle tones, ever, and now the kindness came very easily to him): "I am pleased to see you both so happy, really. This is the best day of my whole life."

"We were listening to the music," Bradley said. "It's...hypnotic. The rhythm of it..."

Babajee was delighted. He said happily: "The marriage dance... With his right hand, each of the dancers is driving away the unhappiness that is in his left, and each little clap that you hear is the death of another spirit of evil."

Petna looked up at Bradley, her face alive with pleasure. She said: "And soon, there will be no evil left for any of us. There will only be happiness."

Her world was here, in this house and in the shaded garden where the seven-year moonflower was blooming this night, and the scent of the frangipani was heady and intoxicating.

Outside, not too far away, there were terrible questions that had to be answered; there were Africans burning the *dukas* down and creeping through the fields with long knives; but here, on her arm, there was only the man she was to marry.

The beat of the sticks was hypnotic.

They clutched them above their heads, the dancing men, and moved in a slow rhythmic circle to the thin sound of a reed pipe, moving three paces forward, then swinging around abruptly to clap their twin sticks against those of the men behind them, then swinging forward again with wide-paced steps to strike at the sticks in front, striking always high over their heads, swinging their shoulders slowly, clapping them together in a drowsy cadence. But the sweat poured from their faces and soiled their neat white shirts, and as the tempo increased and they moved faster and faster, the slow steps became hops, and then little rapid jumps, and soon it seemed that the shining floor was shaking with the rhythm of them.

Round and round they moved, the circle growing tighter, and the Indians watched attentively and the English fiddled uncomfortably with their drinks.

The Indian girl who was to dance later was sitting in a darkened corner, her hand moving impulsively as Cassel tried surreptitiously to caress her thigh; there was a small red spot painted in the center of her forehead, and her eyes were darkened with *kohl,* against which a single gold ornament at the bridge of her nose swung brightly, catching the light every time she moved. Her bodice was gold-braided, dark green and shining, too, tight to the neck but showing a broad band of warm flesh at the waist above her long skirt. She could not speak English at all, and as she fumbled at Cassel's exploring hand she kept muttering: "*Hapana! Bado, bado!*" and glancing across at Babajee and at the other Indians.

Only Bradley was unaware of the tenseness in the atmosphere. He watched the Greeks gathering into tight little circles, talking their business; and the Indians tending to break up their own tight circles to talk to the English; and the rest of the Englishmen and their wives trying hard to enjoy themselves and wondering why they bothered, feeling grateful at least for the liquor...feeling that another day was passing on the intolerable route to a future that could only be a question mark for all of them.

Bradley looked about him, beaming, knowing that here was a victory, a personal victory for himself and all that he stood for, not even wondering if the elation he felt was partly political, sure that his happiness was all that counted because he stood for an integration of all peoples, and that one of the races had been advanced a little by the affairs of his own heart.

Like the others, he had drunk too much of Babajee's whiskey, and he tried hard not to let his speech show it; he spoke slowly, laboriously, carefully, choosing his words and not being aware of the long pauses while he searched for lucidity.

He said to Petna, smiling at her, unaware of the incongruity: "The Englishman...the one thing the Englishman hates...is change, did you know that? Change. He wants the status quo, even if it's bad. And yet...the emotions are always the same, and all we have to do is to guide them into the proper channels, to make them serve a purpose. It's only the mind that differs, and the mind...it can be changed much more easily and, by God, we're changing it, do you realize that?"

Petna's eyes were very solemn, not understanding, knowing that he was drunk and accepting it.

He said thickly: "This is the first...the first interracial marriage in the Colony, did you know that? Except for the Greeks, of course."

He looked at Gregory obliquely, but Gregory only waved a cheerful hand at him. Gregory's wife was an African, but he kept her hidden well away, and most of the guests in his hotel assumed she was merely the cook.

He said: "Well, you know what I mean... The mind is changing all the time, environment, heredity... It's only the emotions... I came out here quite sure that the answer to the African problem was a simple one; it's brotherly love, by God, a thing they've been preaching for God knows how long, and no one's paid any attention to it. It just shows you..." There was a long pause again while he tried to remember what he was saying.

"The emotions," he said at last, "if we could channel those too... They say the clash is bound to come, but is it? I don't believe it is. If we can show willing..."

She could not hide the touch of dismay on her face, and when she saw that he had noticed it, she said quickly, making a joke of it: "Are you marrying me to prove a point? Is that it?"

He swayed a little on his feet and said: "That's the trouble with women, they're too damned...illogical. I'm marrying you because...because I love you, it's as simple as that. It just happens that..." He looked ruefully at his glass and said: "And when we're married, I shall expect you to put your foot down once in a while. I shouldn't drink so much."

The orchestra stopped, and there was polite applause. The dancers tugged at their collars and perspired.

When she laughed, he could feel her body moving, a slight inclination at the incredibly slender waist, almost as if there were no spine there to hold the torso rigid but only a gentle hourglass of soft flesh that swayed like a flower with the most delicate touch of the wind. She pulled at the twist of the sari at her waist, and he looked at her gravely and said: "You're the most beautiful woman I have ever seen. How can I look at you and talk about...about the emotions? They're irrational, aren't they?... But...this is a rational, irrational affair... Does that make sense? No, I suppose it doesn't."

She turned away as her father crossed over to the orchestra and gave the signal to start again, and the panting men in the center of the room began to move slowly around in their circle, once more clapping their sticks behind their backs, then in front to one side and then to the other, and then above the heads, and then, with a sudden turn, striking the sticks of the men behind them, all moving together in little jerky steps, like the threatening paces of Satarkarni warriors advancing into battle against the troopers of the Mauryan Empire. Each pace was a beat of the drum, each turn a sudden start of passion, and the clash of the sticks, the short staccato sound of them, began its hypnotic beat against Bradley's senses, pounding into him.

He found himself fascinated, watching the feet, waiting for the quick turn, waiting for the beat, waiting for the sudden, sharp movement that was telling an age-old story that he could not understand.

When he began to speak, he saw that Petna, too, was watching, her eyes half-closed, and soon he was aware that she had left him; her body was still tight beside him, but when he pressed her waist with a gentle pressure there was no answering movement from her; and in a little while there was nothing in the world but the unceasing metronome of the sticks.

He knew that until he died, every time he heard that beat he would think of her.

"But why?" Petna asked incredulously. "Why? You don't have to put up with him like this."

Cassel was fast asleep on one of the big old-fashioned brass beds, his shirt open at the neck, his thin, aristocratic features bloated. One of the African servants was impassively removing his shoes.

Marion sat on the edge of the bed and looked at him and said: "It's a good question. But if you've ever been in love..."

"Even when he treats you like this? You saw how he was pawing at that girl. A dancing girl!"

Marion said savagely: "The way some women hang onto their husbands... Yes, I could leave him, I suppose. But I'd be back again as soon as..." She bit her lip and said: "He knows I can't manage without him. He knows. It's stupid, isn't it? Twenty of my friends downstairs and I've been to bed with every man jack of them, and still... When he's sober, there's nobody like him." She looked up at

Petna and said: "When you're older, you'll know just where your heart is. It's between your legs. That's all there is to it." She got up wearily and said: "He'll sleep for a while, and then he'll find his own way home, and he'll be sick all over the carpet... You may well ask why the bloody hell I put up with it."

"And you?"

Marion went to the mirror on the ornate marble dressing table and patted her hair into place. Not looking at Petna, she said: "A better man than...than that is waiting for me."

It was a week later.

The moon was low in the sky against the flat tops of the thorn trees, and the air was cold as they came up the gravel track out of the Rift Valley and hit the asphalt fast in Gerald Scott's Jaguar.

A round mud-and-wattle hut was on the edge of the bluff above them, and as Gerald began to pull over to the side of the road, with the wide floor of the valley spread out far beneath them, filled with silent, invisible predatory animals, she put a hand on his arm and said quietly: "Not here. Further on."

He looked at her and grinned, then swung the car back onto the road.

"So why don't we go over to my place?"

"I've got a job to do." Her voice was slurred.

"A job?"

"I'm going to fix that bastard I married. For good."

He was never quite sure of her when she was drunk. He put a hand on her knee, slipping it along the inside of her thigh.

"We could use the guesthouse..."

"I'm going to fix him."

He did not understand her, but he shrugged it off, wondering how much she'd been drinking that night.

They were coming to the fork in the road and he slowed down again, stopped at the angle, switched off the lights, looked at her, dropped his look to the white flesh above the line of her dress, and said: "We could romp around on the bed for a couple of hours and still get you back before daylight. It's a good night for love, I'm

61

strong tonight, strong as a bloody ramrod."

He put an arm around her and slipped a hand between her legs again, marveling at the softness of her flesh, wanting her badly. But she pulled away from him and flipped down the mirror over the visor, looking at her hair and grimacing. "Give me your comb."

He sighed and pulled a comb out of his hip pocket, handing it to her and then reaching for the silver flask that was under the dash. He gestured at her with it and when she shook her head he took a swig from it, put it back, and waited patiently. He had never known her so cold and controlled, even in drunkenness, and when she opened the door and stepped out he leaned over in surprise and said: "What goes on...? Let's get over among the bushes at least."

She looked for a moment down the long gravel road towards her house, bright-lit by the moonlight, framed in acacias and poplars, and then she turned back to him and said, her voice very low: "Pull off the road and wait for me. If anyone comes, drive off a bit and then come back here. Keep your eyes open."

Puzzled, he blinked at her.

"If you'd only tell me what you're up to... Wait for you? What then?"

"Then...we'll go home."

"You're the boss."

He thrust aside the moment of awkwardness and said: "I only hope you're not going to tell him...about us."

There was genuine amusement on her face. "Tell him? Good God Almighty, you think he doesn't know? You really think that?"

He said in sudden alarm: "Well, I hope he doesn't...for God's sake..."

"He knows, Gerald, he knows. And he doesn't give a monkey's brass arse about it. He knows about you, and about all the others as well. At least, about some of them. So just sit here like a good boy and wait for Mama, all right?"

He stared at her, and she was gone.

He shrugged away the nagging worry and watched her slim body moving away on the dusty road till the darkness hid it. He lit a cigarette. It tasted sour and he threw it away, took another drink, moved into the back, put his feet up on the front seat, and closed his eyes.

Far below in the valley the hyenas were calling, a hundred or more of them, pack-hunting; he lowered the window and listened to them for a moment, hearing even the galloping sound of their hooves, like horses. He could smell the sweet scent of wood smoke coming from the village on the crest of the hill, and somewhere a bush baby barked, and then he slept for a while and when he opened his eyes and looked at his watch he was astonished to see that half an hour had gone by.

He muttered angrily to himself and stepped out of the car, wondering if she'd ditched him and not understanding why she should want to do a thing like that, and then he saw her, far down the road, coming towards him slowly, walking in the shadows of the trees at the side of the oleander hedge.

He went towards her and said: "I was worried. Thought you weren't coming back."

She stooped and took off one of her spike-heeled shoes, holding onto his arm while she tipped the sand out of it. She said inconsequentially: "It's hell walking in sand with high-heeled shoes."

He hesitated and then said: "Did you go home? Was he there?"

She said clearly: "How should I know where he is? I just went into the bushes..."

"For half an hour?"

"More like five minutes. You must be drunk."

There was an edge to her voice that startled him, but then she smiled quickly, reaching up and putting a hand at the back of his head, drawing his lips down to hers. He pulled her body tight against him, feeling the firm outline of her breasts and the sweep of her thigh.

He put his mouth close to her ear and said: "Shall we go to my place? Please? Please, Marion... I need you so badly...so very badly..." When she did not answer, he put a careful note of urgency into his voice and tried to force some tears into his eyes. He blinked at her humbly and said: "Please, my darling, if you only knew the great need I have... It's something...something I can't control..." He thought to himself: *Bloody hell, what's the matter with her tonight, she's going to say no, the cold-blooded bitch.* He said: "Please? To my place?"

She kissed him again and then pulled away, straightening her

63

dress. "No. Let's go to my house."

Startled, not knowing whether to be pleased or surprised, he said: "But...what about...won't he...?"

"He'll be dead drunk, as usual. Dead drunk on the living room sofa, with a bottle of good Scotch all over the floor. Just like any other night."

"All right, but..." He raised a hopeless hand. "It might be a hell of a lot safer at my place, and we can be there in ten minutes. Too many bloody guns in that house of yours, and you can never quite trust a white hunter, they're too bloody quick with them."

"Frightened, Gerald? Of that drunken bastard?"

He said roughly: "No, I'm not. Let's go." He opened the car door for her, and drove off in an angry, sullen silence to her house.

The white wooden gates were locked, and she did not speak when he got down and unlocked them (leaving them open for a hurried getaway, should it be necessary), and when he got back into the car he looked at the smooth, relaxed line of her shoulders and thought: *What the hell, if he does catch us, who cares, it's worth it, the hell with it.* He wished he could have another drink, but the idea of the gesture disturbed him—*taking out a flask for a quick drink before you get into bed with a pretty woman, not quite the thing, old boy...* He said, instead: "Where shall I park?"

"Outside the front door, where else?"

"Are you sure, Marion? I don't care how drunk he is, he can't be out cold, I mean not absolutely *cold.* Why don't we leave the car around the back...?"

She did not answer, and he sighed and left the Jaguar in the driveway, then waited while she looked in her evening bag for the key. She smiled at him quickly as she unlocked the door, a sudden, sparkling smile that reminded him of a mischievous schoolgirl.

An image flashed across his mind, something she had told him, laughing, a long time ago: "Her name was Miss Proctor, a disappointed virgin, and this boy, what the hell was his name, all muscle and all in the right places..." She had giggled then, and said: "I'll never forget my father's face when she told him..." And suddenly, the smile had gone and she had said soberly: "He was such a good man, my father." He had been startled to see that she was

64

suddenly almost crying, the schoolgirl giggle gone so fast that it was already an illusion. She had said again: "Such a good man."

She threw open the front door and switched on the hall lights, and called out loudly:

"Mohammed! Mohammed?"

Gerald's spirits dropped to a sudden despair. He said angrily: "What the hell do we want with the servants?"

She said calmly: "I want some coffee. Wouldn't do you any harm, either. And don't be so damn churlish when you can't get what you want when you want it."

She called again, louder: "Mohammed! *Umesikia?*"

The kitchen door opened, and Mohammed was there, his eyes sleep-rimmed, his white teeth showing in a broad grin. He said happily: "*Nimesikia, Memsahib...*"

"Well, make some coffee. Where's the *Bwana?*"

"*Kule, Memsahib.*" With a faint gesture, he indicated the living room door. "*Mbili? Tatu?*"

"Three. Coffee for three."

The old servant nodded and moved silently back to the kitchen.

Gerald said sullenly: "Three o'clock in the morning and we have a bloody party, husband and all. And I bet he's so bloody drunk he won't even know we're here."

The lights were on in the big living room, and Cassel was sprawled across the sofa on his stomach, one hand limply hanging down as though reaching for the empty bottle that had rolled across the floor. His lank hair hung down over his forehead, and he had taken off his shoes because they hurt his feet; there was a hole in one of the white socks.

Marion said disgustedly: "For God's sake...wake him up, Gerald."

He said quietly: "Can't we...do we have to...?"

"Wake him up."

He sighed. He took Cassel by the shoulder and shook him, pulling him around into a sitting position, saying with forced good humor: "All right, old boy, time to get up, time to wash the baby."

Cassel's head fell forward loosely, and Gerald stared and gasped and stared again, and then said stupidly: "I believe...I

65

think...for God's sake...!"

He pulled at the shoulder again and the head fell back, thrusting out the Adam's apple, then toppled over sideways, quite loosely, at an angle that was almost comic.

Gerald looked up at Marion and saw that she was staring at him, her eyes cold, composed and almost blank. He said thickly: "His neck's broken. So that's... My God, my God Almighty..."

The drunkenness had gone and there was a terrible clarity in its place. He felt that his face was white.

Marion looked at him and said very clearly: "So that's what, Gerald?" And then, in the same breath, she began to scream, and when Mohammed came running in she shrieked: "He's dead, Mohammed, the *Bwana's* dead."

Gerald sank down in a chair and put his head in his hands, only vaguely, very far away, hearing Mohammed speak on the phone to the duty sergeant at the police station. He dropped his hands limply between his knees, stared at the whiskey bottle on the floor, and waited.

Marion went to the couch by the window, curled up in one corner of it, pulled back the drapes with a perfectly steady hand, and stared out into the darkness.

PART TWO

The People of Jesus Christ, Esquire

CHAPTER 5

But outside the restricting confines of the towns, the true Africa was still unknown.

The bush had been hunted over, trampled, explored; but it was unknown because the men who had built the Continent had never stayed there for very long. Where there was water, or a defensive site that could be held against the raiders who had struggled to assert themselves over the ages, or where a road could be built to follow the old elephant tracks from one river to another, they had put down their roots and towns had grown. But in the bush country they went swiftly or slowly from one oasis of stability to another, from one remote farm to the next, seldom staying long enough in the thirsty desert to learn that here, in the wilderness where hardly anyone lived, there was a vast and empty land that a man could easily love, in spite of all about it that was harsh, and lonely, and savage.

Willis had said, and there was excitement in his voice: "There's a report come in about a herd of dibatag up in the Northern Frontier District. You know about the dibatag? The best of all the gazelles, and they're supposed to be dying out, close to extinction, and now they say there's a herd been sighted, over a thousand strong. A thousand of them in one herd! Can you believe that?"

In the neat white bungalow that Tabor had bought, surrounded with the bright green of the coffee bushes and the tangled trailers of wild strawberry, Willis spread his map over the highly polished surface of the teak table and stabbed at it with wiry fingers.

"Here, up here somewhere, nothing but hot desert and a few

67

scattered water holes, and all the animals in creation... You want to come along?" He added carefully: "An extra rifle just might be useful."

Tabor looked across the purple mountains that dropped, in ever-lowering ranges, one after the other away from the high peak of the homestead; somewhere out there the hot desert was a long way off. He stared at the map somberly and nodded. "More than a year since I was out in the bush, and that's where the real Africa is. Sure, I'll be glad to get out there again."

"Good. Then we'll leave on Monday." Willis smiled slowly and said: "And Marion Cassel is coming too—she wants to get some photographs of the herd. If we find it."

Tabor reached for the bourbon bottle and said lightly: "Well, that'll be nice." He looked at Willis and frowned. "I suppose she knows that the Jesus boys are up there."

"She knows." Willis snorted his contempt and said: "And that's something you'll have to learn sooner or later if you're going to stay here; they're just one of the little problems that crop up from time to time; we learn to live with them."

The green-painted Land Rover was a tiny speck on an immense, sun-baked desert, followed by its own cloud of dust that looked like a saffron plume trailing behind it.

As far as you could see there was nothing but yellow sand, with gray-green scrub that tightly hugged the earth in scattered patches, with an occasional thorn tree that towered high above everything else, its broad green top spreading out like an umbrella as though breathing deeply now that it had climbed so far above the stifling, dusty sand.

Gray-green and yellow-gray was the color, speckled and dappled, and it stretched from the escarpment clear down to the sea, where the coarse flat sand changed to jagged, broken cliffs.

The land was so beautiful that you caught your breath when you first looked at it; you knew why men would grow to love it with a peculiar intensity, and you knew, too, why they would fight to keep their hold on it.

The silence here was so absolute that you could think you had left the world behind, that Africa was not part of the earth at all, but on the inhospitable surface of some remote and hostile planet. The silence was so absolute that when the three shots came, fired one after the other in rapid succession, Marion slammed on the brakes, sending the unbalanced boys in the back sprawling over each other, and she said, startled: "What was that?"

Willis said calmly, because he was worrying about it: "Three shots, that's what it was."

For the last six days of their journey, the ugly rumors had met them in the widely scattered villages. At first, the reports were clear and recounted with scorn because the danger was far away. But soon the scorn had gone, though the clarity had remained, and the tales were tinged with fear instead. And as they drove deeper into the bush the villagers were more and more frightened, so frightened at the last that they stayed in their huts as the truck pulled in to replenish its water supply.

Now, Tabor said dryly: "There was a time, once, when rifle fire meant someone was out hunting."

"Not that kind of fire, it's too fast, there's no time to aim. Over there, somewhere, down in the valley."

The valley was a great abrupt cleft in the surface of the earth that ran from the mountains clear down to the sea. Marion had already swung the nose of the Land Rover around toward it, heading for the edge of the steep sandstone precipice at its edge, moving fast towards the sound that could only mean trouble. She hugged the wheel, crouching over it, her green shirt sleeves rolled up, her brown arms showing the faint blond hairs; there was a grease stain on the thigh of her tight khaki trousers.

She grimaced and jerked her head towards the back of the truck, and said laconically: "They're worried."

Willis turned to look at the two Africans. Their faces were inscrutable. He smiled quickly and said in Swahili: "Nothing to be afraid of. We have guns."

Adoula, the elder of the two, nodded his head. M'toto, the young one, shivered and hoped no one would notice.

Willis turned back to the others and said softly: "Don't anyone mention their name, or the boys will up and run. We may need them."

ALAN CAILLOU

"Bloody black savages," Tabor said without rancor. "Get my hands on them I'll teach them a thing or two about Communion. Blood of the Lamb! For Christ's sake!"

"Don't say it!" Willis insisted. "They can guess too, but as long as they're not sure... Come to that, we could be wrong too."

They came to the valley in a little while, and stopped the truck at the edge of the sheer-seeming drop that fell away to its bed. The sun was behind them now, and the sandstone cliff had turned to purple in the shadows.

When they clambered out to take a look, Willis pointed a wiry brown arm and said: "Over there. The bus."

They could see it clearly, far below them on the twin ribbon of the wheel ruts that served as a road across this vast emptiness, a crude track that wound unaccountably from side to side, in and out among the thorn trees. Close by a clump of giant acacias, the bright yellow bus was an odd anachronism, out of time and out of place too. Through the glasses, they examined it carefully, looking for any sign of life; there was nothing.

Marion was standing, her arms akimbo, her legs straddled like a man, looking down into the chasm, her long yellow hair streaming down over her shoulder; the fine lines on her face were dark with dust that had settled in them.

She sighed and said: "I suppose if we just point the truck in the right direction we could slide down to the bottom. Can't guarantee we'd get there in one piece, though."

"Leave it here and walk," Willis said.

Tabor answered: "The hell with that. Let's try it."

Willis sighed, and his eyes were troubled.

Marion looked at him and knew that the sigh was not for the difficult drive down the cliff but for what they might find when they reached the bus, and she touched him lightly on the shoulder and said: "Perhaps it's nothing. Perhaps they just broke down, heard the sound of our motor, and fired to attract our attention."

It would have been pointless to have said: *So, then where are they now?* Instead, he looked silently through the glasses again, searching out the bushes around the bus, looking at the cluster of giant boulders that stood a little way away from it, the quartz in them giving out a gleam that was almost eerie.

He turned back then and said simply: "So let's see what we can do. What are we waiting for?"

The two Africans were already moving the baggage in the back, ramming it down tight and pulling a rope over the boxes of food, strapping the bedding more firmly to the metal sides.

"Shall I drive?" Willis stood by the wheel and waited, and when Marion shook her head, he said: "At least, we'd better walk beside you, see if we can find a way down..."

She clambered into the truck and they watched as she eased it over the edge, admiring her expertise.

The Land Rover stood almost on its nose for an instant, and Adoula squealed and then grinned broadly, showing his shining white teeth as it slithered for fifty feet and came to a stop against a hand of roots that had forced their way out of the earth. The slope below them was alarming.

Marion looked back over her shoulder and shouted: "Only one way to go now, and that's down..."

They dropped on foot down the steep slope beside her, putting their shoulders to the back of the truck and heaving, and when it moved again it slid around sideways and went down fast, twisting drunkenly, dangerously, and Marion wrestled with the wheel and righted it again, and then it was off like a wild thing, bouncing madly down a sixty-degree slope until it seemed that it must surely turn over.

Tabor was jumping down as fast as he could move, his muscled arms outstretched, his dark face wet with perspiration. He fell once and rolled over, and the first thing he did after he got up was to swear volubly and examine the breech mechanism of his Mauser .306, dusting the sand from it and looking back at Willis with a grin.

The two Africans were enjoying themselves now, slithering down after the Land Rover like children, on their behinds, and laughing, forgetting the question that waited for them, knowing only that at this moment they were finding delight in the fragmentary loss of their dignity. Willis marveled, as he always marveled, at the speed with which the troublesome thoughts could leave them—and come back again too. For them it was not that *tomorrow* did not matter; it was that anything beyond the immediate minute was of no consequence at all; the worries would come, and they could be faced when they did. It was an age-old philosophy that was peculiarly African.

The Land Rover had shuddered to a stop. The bus was a mile or two away from them, a bright yellow splash in the desert, the setting sun reflecting itself on the windshield; it seemed to be tilted over to one side. Only the birds broke the silence, and when Willis spoke, his voice was heavy and tired.

"Let's go and take a look at it. But don't stop until I give the word, keep the truck rolling. Keep your guns handy and be ready to move out, fast."

What had happened to this country he loved so well? For fifty years and more it had been his home, the only home he had ever known, the only home he had ever wanted, because here, amid the scrub and the jungle, in the dry wastes and the overwatered forests, in the flat deserts and the broken mountains, there was all that any man could ever want; there was a great life here for a man whose intimacies were with the lavish legacy of nature, for a man to whom space, and beauty, and the clean air, and the great silence, and the true well-being of simplicity were all that really counted.

It was not the first occasion... From time to time, here in the equatorial east of a continent that had known violence through the run of its history, that violence had sometimes sprung to sudden, savage life, and then died down again in lethargy and was forgotten.

But this time... Was it once again in isolation? Or was it all part of a vast and changing pattern that he could not understand because of the shock of its consistency? This time, it was not here alone, it was all around him; everywhere the outbreaks had taken their predictable course, but this time they were all happening at once and the pattern had become gross and frightening.

The fine sand spurted out from under the tires as the truck shot forward, racing fast over the broken ground, its attendant powdery plume hanging high in the motionless air behind it. And when they reached the old bus they drove around it twice in narrowing circles, choking on their own dust. There was not a breath of air down here, though the valley led, thirty miles to the east, down to the cool waters of the coast.

They drove around the bus again, slower now, and when Marion said "Nothing..." Tabor jerked a calloused thumb towards it and said: "Look out for a wire." A long steel cable, stolen perhaps from an Army store, was twisted around one of the front wheels, cutting deeply into the radiator; the water still dripped lazily into the thirsty sand, and one end of the cable was wound around the trunk of a thorn tree.

When Marion braked to a halt, Tabor jumped quickly down, pulled his rifle from the gun rack, and said brusquely: "Cover me."

Willis said: "Wait." He jerked his head at Marion and said: "Take the shotgun." There was authority in his voice, and they waited till he was ready and then the three of them walked towards the bus together in a thin, watchful line, their eyes alert, their movements smooth and easy, moving like soldiers, armed and in open order.

The bus was an old American truck, a Dodge, about fifteen years old, with a carpenter-built wooden body on it that was meant to hold twenty or twenty-five crowded Africans on narrow benches down both sides of the open back. The roof was piled high with accusing bundles, pathetically abandoned; a terra-cotta jar that was wedged in among them had cracked open and was leaking rancid butter over the sides. The rear tires, worn down to the canvas, were patched with hunks of rubber that had been fastened in place with iron bolts, and there were two small round holes in the strapped-on emergency gasoline tank, below which the sand was stained with a tinge of pink. "Army gas," Tabor said, meaning the pink dye that was put in it to make it harder to steal.

Willis was staring at the name that was painted in red letters on the wooden body: R.U. BABAJEH, NORTHERN FRONTIER TRANSPORTATION. He put a hand on the motor; it was cold. There was only silence around them.

Marion stared out into the bush, avoiding Willis' eye, and when she said, making conversation: "I wonder where they went..." Tabor pointed to the rocks that were half a mile away and said: "Over there. Where else?"

Willis blinked his eyes and Marion touched his arm and said gently: "It might have been just the driver."

Willis said harshly: "He drives the bus himself."

"Then he was probably...alone. Who knows?"

They heard the sharp sound as Tabor worked the breech of his rifle, and stared at the rocks which were suddenly his target. His rifle, its barrel incredibly motionless, was pointing towards them, and Willis put out a hand and said urgently: "Wait, it's probably Babajee..." But then the shadow over there moved, and a man was moving into sight, a white man, a tiny figure in the distance, waving his hat at them and running forward.

Tabor lowered his gun and said disgustedly: "It's that jerk Bradley. What's he doing out here?" His eyes were good, hunter's eyes that could keep the V of the sights on a running animal's neck at three hundred yards or more.

The figure grew and staggered towards them, and when it reached them it dropped to its knees as though in prayer, its hands hanging down at its sides with the fingers downward, pointing into the unfriendly soil, and Willis said sharply: "Bradley! Where's your rifle? Was it you who fired?"

Bradley swayed on his knees as though he would collapse, and a stifled sob went through him. Willis looked at him with distaste.

He was out of breath, panting heavily, his lungs bursting. He stammered, searching for the words: "I left it...with Baba and the...the women...the others..."

"The women?" Willis was suddenly savagely angry.

Marion looked at him and said nothing, feeling his pain.

Bradley nodded, his hair falling over his face, then dropped forward till the palms of his hands were on the sand at their feet. There was a touch of hysteria on him. He said, shuddering: "There were thirty or forty of them...of the *watu*, with guns and...spears, and *pangas*... They stopped the truck... Oh, God, dear God, I'd never have believed it..."

Willis leaned down and grabbed his shoulder and yanked him forcibly to his feet and shouted angrily: "Pull yourself together. What women?"

Bradley shook his head and said, stuttering: "Two African women...passengers on the bus. And Petna."

"Are they hurt? Are they all right?" He forced a calm into his voice. "Where are they now?"

Bradley turned and pointed. "Over there... We took cover in the rocks. We just had...one gun..."

"And the *watu?*"

The fear was robbing Bradley of his speech. Tabor spat into the sand and said sourly: "All right, junior, where are the Jesus boys?"

Bradley looked up and there was venom on his face, but he could not keep it there. "They disappeared. We heard your truck and I fired to signal you, and then...they were gone, all of them. Nothing." He spread his hands hopelessly and repeated; "Nothing. Thirty or forty of them, and...nothing."

He looked around at the unfriendly desert, vast, silent, empty, unable to believe that it had so easily swallowed them up, so easily afforded hiding places for thirty or forty savages, triumphantly rampaging terrorists.

Marion went over to the Land Rover, took out the whiskey bottle, and handed it to Bradley without a word. She did not like him very much, and when he saw the disdain on her face he began to refuse it, then changed his mind and muttered: "I could do with a drink." He took a swig from the bottle and wiped his hand across his mouth.

Tabor said dryly, not trying to hide the contempt: "Feel like telling us what happened? If you're up to it, of course."

Bradley ignored him. He turned to Willis and said: "What the hell could I do? Just one rifle between us." He was ashamed of himself now, shamed by Marion's tight-lipped silence. He looked around in embarrassment and said: "I was over in the village, in Mwadi, to see the chief, and...there were three of them there, three of the *watu...*"

"How did you know? They wear a goddam uniform?"

He looked at Tabor resentfully and said: "They weren't trying to hide it. They'd come in for supplies, and the villagers...the villagers were afraid of them, and...I tried to arrest them, all three of them, but some of the young men started objecting, and threw stones at me, and when I ran...a riot started..."

Willis said incredulously: "You *ran?*"

"Well, of course, I had to, they were stoning me..."

"And you're surprised a riot started?" Tabor said with a snort.

"Run from these bastards, it's all they want to show them they're as good as they think they are. Your bloody black brothers."

Bradley said furiously: "It's men like you who turn them against us! If you'd have a little...a little respect for them...if you'd remember they haven't had the chances that you've had, that they...all they want is to be treated like men, not like animals..."

"Oh, shut up, for Christ's sake." Tabor turned away and Bradley's voice spluttered to silence. He said resentfully: "Men like him."

Willis sighed and said mildly: "He's entitled to his viewpoint." He said to Bradley: "What happened when you ran? The riot?"

"They turned my truck over and set fire to it, and..." There was the uncomfortable gesture again, a hand raised hopelessly in the air as though grasping for assurance that he had done all that he could be expected to do. "I ran from the village, and there was Baba's bus coming in, just a few African passengers aboard, and Petna, and I stopped him and turned it back, and we headed out of there, fast... It was all right until we got here, and then the bus ran into a cable across the track, and there was the main body of them, thirty, forty, maybe more, in broad daylight, out in the open..."

"Any guns?"

"Yes. They had...four or five rifles. One of them had a pistol, a Luger. The others had spears, bows and arrows, *pangas*... We jumped out of the bus and started to run for cover of the rocks over there, and...they killed three or four of the Africans... One of them went down on his knees and started praying to them and they...they cut his head off, one slash with a *panga*, it was... Oh God, it was awful."

Willis had gone a little apart from them and was searching the bush with his sharp, pale eyes.

Tabor said, turning back to Bradley: "The women?"

"There were only a few passengers," Bradley said, "seven or eight Africans, two of them had their wives with them. Baba was driving. There was one other Indian... He disappeared, I don't know what happened to him...and...there was his daughter..." He swallowed hard and said: "There was Petna, too, sitting beside her father in the bus. I tried to cover them as they ran for shelter, as best I could...just the one rifle..." His voice trailed off miserably, and when he looked around nervously, recovering his coherence and his fears at the same time, Willis looked over his shoulder at him.

Willis said: "How long ago?"

"Three, four hours." Bradley looked at his watch. "We left the village at half past one and ran into the ambush about an hour later. Three hours ago, a little more."

"And then?"

"I kept them away from the rocks with my rifle... I shot two of them, I think..."

"You think? Don't you *know?*"

Bradley took another drink of the whiskey and said: "Well, I *think* I did, I'm not sure. They were hiding out among the bushes, trying to creep up on us, and...it was hard to be sure. And when we heard your truck up on the escarpment, I fired three shots to attract your attention."

"And they left then?"

"I...I don't know. When I looked out again, there was nothing there. Nothing. They'd just...disappeared." He looked around nervously again, feeling the danger still there, and said defiantly: "I've only got eight rounds left."

Tabor was circling the bus, looking alternately into the bush and down at the ground at his feet. He found a brown stain and touched it with his fingers, and smelled the blood and looked hard into the bushes, seeing the marks in the sand where a body had been dragged and knowing that it would no longer be there, not so close by, but hidden away as though the things to be perpetrated on it were not to be seen by man, but only by God, by their particular God...

There were movements now in the distance over among the rocks, a small group peering out at them and waiting.

Tabor went and stood by Willis and said slowly: "Not a sign of anything. A few drops of blood is all." A pause. "They could be waiting for us out there somewhere."

"We are too well armed and they know it." Willis was satisfied that the *watu* were no longer there. He swung his rifle onto his shoulder, gripping it by the barrel, and turned to Tabor and said: "Let's go and get them." The deep lines at the corners of his mouth were taut, and his eyes were clouded, as though he were trying to shield his thoughts from them.

Marion turned her back on Bradley and went over to Willis and said, speaking very quietly: "She's all right, Willis. If she'd been hurt, he'd have said so, you know that."

For a little while, Willis stared at the sand and did not speak, and then he turned to her very slowly and looked at the compassion in her eyes and said wearily: "I didn't know that you knew."

"I knew. I've known for a long time." She said again: "She's all right, Willis."

Together, they walked over to the truck.

His heart was heavy when he saw her. She looked so frail and...scared, scared out of her wits. It was almost more than she could do to control herself, to stop herself from running to him with open arms, to say, sobbing: *Thank God, Willis, thank God you're here...* And on that smooth-skinned, wide-eyed, emotional face, it showed.

He worried, as always, lest her father should understand what was between them, of what had been between them for a long time now. But they had kept the secret well, though she was uncomfortable about it, even after Bradley, two years ago now, had come upon the scene and taken her away from him.

"I will never stop loving you," she had said, clutching at him with her supple, delicate arms; he could feel the sharp nails digging into his bare flesh. "Only...my father...what he wants me to do, I must do."

"Marry that little squirt Bradley?" he had said scornfully. "He must be out of his mind. What happened to all those racial prejudices? A Punjabi girl with a white man for a husband? There's not an Indian in his community will let him get away with it."

"That's not true. Times are changing."

"Changing for him, but not for you, is that it?" A note of anger had crept into his voice. "Your father can marry you off outside his caste, outside his creed, outside his color, but still...he's still the one who chooses your husband, just like in the old days. It doesn't make sense."

"None of the old prejudices make sense. But, when you destroy them, that doesn't make sense either."

He rolled over on his hack in the dry sand at the edge of the surf, his feet just reaching the tiny waves that rolled slowly up the beach. He softened, felt tender toward her. "Your skin is cool brown ice, on fire, alive," he said.

"And yours is strong, and scarred, and...resistant."

"You're too young, Petna. I'm old enough to be your grandfather."

"Don't talk like that."

"But I am. If my son had lived..."

She said, urging him to forget: "Think about the life in your veins, not about death."

She waited a little while, feeling the hot sun on her back, lying close to him with her fine bare breast touching his, knowing how much he loved her, knowing how fine it was for him to make love to her like this, on the barren open beach with the sea making the soft noises.

She said very quietly: "I want to have your baby."

For a long time he did not answer her. He knew how much it would mean to him, and to her, and yet... He said at last, kissing her: "No. You know that's impossible."

"But I *want* to."

"And you know we can't. We mustn't. Ever. If we did...your father... You won't defy him over Bradley, and yet...you'd do a thing like that?"

"It would force the issue," she said slowly. "I cannot defy my father willingly. Yet, if I had a baby, he would think that... I do not know what he would think. I only know that once it was done there would be no turning back. A course of desperation is easier than...than defiance."

He smiled at her twisted logic, and said: "I believe you really mean that."

"Of course I do."

"And if...if there were these complications...you know that I still would not marry you."

"I know that too." There was no trouble on her, no harshness in her voice. She had long ago resigned herself to his philosophy, and

79

she smiled at him to make sure that he understood this.

"You must love me very much."

"You know that I do."

"You make me feel guilty, Petna."

"There can be no guilt in love."

"And yet you will marry Bradley."

"Because I love my father too, and what he wants, I must do."
She said impetuously: "He is not thinking of my happiness, I know
that. He is thinking of... of a hundred generations, of all of us. He
wants to bring...to bring our two peoples closer together."

He was suddenly tired, older than his years, remembering the
past. Surprisingly, she began to laugh, pulling him from his
melancholy. Then suddenly, she was solemn again, the laughter
passing so suddenly that he wondered if it were merely a mask to
show him, to let him know that she was not always so grave and
thoughtful.

"With Bradley, I promise you, I will never have any children.
And I promise you this, too, when I am married to him, I will come to
you whenever you want me. *If* you want me. Does that make me
shameful?"

"No." He worried about it, worried about sharing her, worried
about the uncleanliness of it, and said: "I don't know. Just now, it
doesn't bear thinking about."

He wanted to tell her that it was not only because of the
children, that the problem was his too, because his whole life had
been built around the premise, accepted without question until quite
recently, of a natural segregation of the races.

"They have their ways," he would say, shrugging it off, "and we
have ours. What's so bad about that?" But he knew, deep inside him,
that this was not the real reason, had never been more than an excuse
to cover up the hurt inside him, the hurt he was hiding from. He knew
that he was holding himself aloof from this personal involvement,
keeping it merely physical because this he could control, but not the
other. He knew he was hurting her to save himself, but his own hurt
was so great that he would not let it come back and take hold of him
again.

And yet, there was a deep love for this solemn, quiet, dark-skinned child-woman that was quite unbearable, unbearable because, at his own demanding, it could only be satisfied in the flesh.

Now she was tired and frightened. He looked at her without emotion, and said to her father, holding out his hand: "Looks like a nasty business. Are you all right?"

The Indian's hand was moist and soft in his. "Yes, Mr. Willis, we are all right. But if it had not been for Mr. Bradley, I do not know what would have happened to us. It is a miracle, isn't it?"

"Maybe. Nobody hurt?" He looked at the Africans, three men and two women, coming to their feet out of respect for him, waiting, trusting in him implicitly because he was a white man, a *Bwana*, a man who would know what to do now.

"Nobody hurt, Mr. Willis. Only the Africans. They killed three of them, you know."

"Yes, I heard."

"I wonder where their bodies can be. I do not see them, do you?"

"They're out there somewhere. Slung up in a tree, heads down. We'll find them."

Babajee made a gesture of disdain at the rifle he was holding. "I scarcely know how to use it, but if we had not had at least one weapon, isn't it?" His voice was soft, sibilant, lisping. He put a hand and patted his daughter on the shoulder, and she moved a trifle closer to him, her eyes cast down and veiled. "And my daughter with me too, I tell you, if it had not been for Mr. Bradley here..."

Bradley came over and took Petna's hand and stood there, like a love-sick schoolboy. Willis turned away.

Tabor said sourly: "Yeah." He looked at Willis and said: "We've got to get this bunch out of here before dark. Pile them three deep in the Land Rover and there still won't be room."

Willis was searching for something to say, trying not to look at Bradley and wanting to send him away. He said at last: "We'll put them back in the bus and tow it, we've got plenty of power."

"Back to the village? That's where the rest of the *watu* will be right now, waiting for us."

"No, down to the coast."

"A night on the beach?"

Marion was emptying sand out of her ankle-length boots. She looked up quickly and said: "Darhuzuni?"

"Darhuzuni, you know it?"

"The old slave house. Yes, I know it."

"It's not more than thirty miles from here. We can get there by dark, spend the night there, and one of us can go for help in the morning." Willis looked at Bradley and said: "Take the Africans back to the bus and cut the cable loose from the wheels. We'll tow you. Give me the shovels from the Land Rover and we'll see if we can find those bodies, give them a burial of some sort."

It was an hour before they cut the steel cable away from the wheels, and when they pulled the last obstinate segment free, Willis and the others came up, walking in twos and threes out of the bush, their bodies wet with perspiration. Babajee was visibly shaken, still trembling, and Petna was crying softly.

When Bradley put aside the wrench he was holding and looked a question, Willis said slowly: "We found them. Three Africans, one Indian."

"One of my people," Babajee said. There was a tremor in his voice. "A man I did not know, a man who came to sell me some hides. He came here from India only two weeks ago, and now..." He blinked his eyes and looked at his daughter.

Willis said again: "We found them. They'd slung them up by the ankles in a thorn tree, and cut open the veins in their necks."

Petna covered her face with her hands, and Tabor said, looking at Bradley and turning his lip back in contempt: "They washed their robes and made them white. In the Blood of the Lamb."

In the silence, they hitched the tow-rope to the bus.

Father Slattery had been the first casualty to the *watu*.

He was a good man. Unlike some of the missionaries, he firmly believed that he had been sent by God to lead the savages into salvation. He taught them, he succored them, he fed them, and one night, when the Mission hall was crowded, he looked over his flock with a great pride on his face and said gently: "It does my heart good to see so many of you come for the Sacrament."

There had been a time when he had worried that the faith he had instilled in *his* Africans, as he called them, had reflected a dependence upon *him* rather than upon the Word that he taught. He worried that perhaps they trusted in him more than they trusted in the God he told them about; but those days had gone, and he was sure now that his perseverance had brought him his just reward, the great rewards of satisfaction in the work he was doing and in the results he had achieved.

In thirty years? Had it really been so long?

He had built the Mission hut—his first—with his bare hands back in those younger days, with no one to help him but two small children. He had planted the wattle stakes deep in the soil, and had tied long horizontal saplings to them with raffia pulled from the sand, and he had pounded mud to a paste with his bare feet (the children laughing because he did it clumsily) and packed it tight about the saplings until there was a six-inch wall, and then he had burned limestone to make a whitewash and had painted it with a brush made, like the roofing fronds, from palm leaves. And when it was all finished he had looked at his handiwork and told the children: "This is now the House of God. Bring your friends, tell them there is food and medicine, and there is a greater thing too—there is learning. I will teach them to read, and to write, and I will teach them the Word of our beloved Lord God."

Slowly, they had begun to come to him. And slowly, he had taught them.

In the passing years, the old hut had fallen down and a new and bigger one had been built, with a beaten-mud floor and a wide veranda over which creepers splashed their bright colors. A Sister had come to help him, but she had long since died, and lay buried in the tiny compound, her grave marked with a cross which two of his Africans had laboriously carved...

He loved his flock with a great and tolerant love; but he was never quite sure, and it troubled him, how much their continued presence at the Mission was due to their search for a faith, and how much of it was simply a matter of convenience, a matter of food, of shelter, of relative ease.

For some of them, at least, it was entirely the search for a faith, but had the good Father known what form that faith was to take, he would not have been so complaisant; and on that hot October night, for some of them, that faith was crystallized.

It could only be found in the body of Father Slattery himself, for to his flock no other man was more holy; they had decided then that the blood of no other could wash away their sins. As the frail old priest knelt at his altar (carved by hand from solid blocks of *mvuli* wood), a young man named Peter Tarutu stood up, called out in a loud voice: *"Now we will drink the Blood of the Lamb,"* and held up the long-bladed knife which he carried in his belt. It was the prearranged signal.

Father Slattery, surprised out of his prayers by the sudden, unexpected commotion behind him, looked around over his thin shoulder, to see a group of them, naked *pangas* in their hands, advancing on him slowly. He began to stumble to his feet, but one of them pushed him down to the floor again, and then they held him there by the arms and legs, kneeling beside him, while Peter Tarutu cut off, first, his ears and nose, then his arms and legs, and finally, with the now-blunted *panga*, his head.

Then, fourteen of them knelt on the bloody floor of the Mission, wiped the blood carefully over their chests and faces, and quietly began to pray. Peter Tarutu led them.

"Thank you, O Lord," he chanted. "Thank you for sending us the Holy Father to show us the way to Salvation..."

One by one, the other Africans in the congregation left the wooden benches that served as pews; some of them crept fearfully away into the night, and some of them came, slowly, to join the kneeling men.

On that October night, the nebulous line that divides the Sacrament from magic lost its adhesion and was shattered.

And, on that October night, the cult was born that soon was to spread with devastating effectiveness through ten thousand square miles of scattered villages and nomadic encampments. Thirty-seven murders were committed in the next three weeks, and before Peter Tarutu was caught and hanged, his followers numbered over three hundred...

They called themselves *watu ya jesu krist eskwa: The People of Jesus Christ, Esquire.*

CHAPTER 6

In spite of their hopes, it was well after sundown when the Land Rover, the great bus lumbering unsteadily along at the end of the rope behind it, pulled up at the crumpled wall that surrounded Darhuzuni on the landward side, hesitated uncertainly for a moment, and then lurched, steaming, through the weed-covered stones and into the compound where the well was.

The old house towered high above them, less ramshackle in the darkness than it might have seemed under the sun. Far below, the silent sea, a silver sheet of immeasurable immensity, with no surf or wave to disturb its placid surface, stretched out from the base of the cliff to the dreamland of the horizon.

They climbed laboriously out of the vehicles and stretched their legs wearily, staring at the deserted, derelict pile of stones that had once been a fine house.

As Bradley began to speak, Marion said sharply: "Be quiet. Listen!"

She was staring up at one of the upper windows, and Willis looked up at it and said, squinting: "There's something there?"

She nodded. "Someone."

"That's a bit unlikely..."

"I am sure. There was a shadow there, too big for an animal, and what the hell's an animal doing on the upper floor of an empty house anyway? There's a man up there."

Their voices were whispers. Tabor said: "Maybe it's occupied, a family."

Willis shook his head. He was one of the few men who had passed this way in recent years. "No. The last owner was an Armenian, but he gave it up years ago, wasn't even fit to camp in."

"It still looks strong enough to hold, with a couple of rifles."

"If the *watu* haven't got here first. But if there's someone there...I think we'd better scout around a bit."

They stood there in the moonlight, the four of them, looking up at the house and wondering, and then Babajee stepped hesitantly with his daughter out of the bus and said nervously: "There's someone there? There can't be... Not unless it's...it's the *watu*. Could they have got here ahead of us? Could they?"

Adoula and the other Africans were standing by the bus, looking up at the window, and then Adoula said suddenly, his voice a hiss in the darkness: "At the side of the house, *Bwana*..."

And when Willis looked back at them, they were suddenly gone, even the women, and he knew they were hiding themselves, not from the fear of what was living but from the fear of what was dead, hiding behind the low stone wall, crouching like predatory animals in the darkness that are ready to run when the odds are too strongly against them. Only Adoula's head was visible above the side of the Land Rover. He was looking at the corner of the building, at a pile of rocks there, his still form scarcely more than a silent shadow, immobile, rocklike.

Willis heard the click of Tabor's rifle. *He won't ask questions,* he thought, *he'll shoot first and find out afterwards what it was he killed...*

He put a restraining hand on Tabor and Tabor growled: "All right, I know, but there's no harm in being careful." He added in a whisper: "That Adoula's got eyes like..."

The shadow at the side of the house moved and came towards them and then spoke. The voice was quiet, restrained, polished, accentless: "Mr. Willis? Is that you, sir?"

"Yes. Who is it?"

They waited, tense in the darkness. Marion was still watching the upper window, leaving the moving shadow at the side of Tabor. The shadow moved again and came forward, became a man.

"John, Mr. Willis. John Carrierco."

87

He wore a dark suit and a heavy overcoat in spite of the heat of the night, and he carried a pair of sunglasses in his hand; as he approached, he slipped the glasses on. Carrierco was one of the new breed of Africans, self-educated by diligence, and quite sure that his emerging Africa needed the strong talents that only men like him could provide. He was the leader of the local Transport Union, a tall, thin man inclined to pomposity.

"We saw your truck, a long way off, but we didn't know who it was."

"We?"

"Juma M'Butu is with me."

Carrierco looked at the bus and worried about it, and Willis said: "They got ambushed by the *watu*."

"My people, Mr. Willis," Carrierco said sadly. "My people. This is why some people still call us, all of us, savages."

His voice betrayed nothing but scorn. He stepped over to Bradley and shook hands, then held out a hand for Marion.

She took it briefly and said dryly: "Only some people. You ran into them too?"

"Yes, they came to the village, and I thought it prudent to leave."

"Like that."

Carrierco shrugged his thin, elegant shoulders. "Chief M'Butu is well known to be their enemy. And after the things he said about them to his men... I heard they were going to take him and I made him leave. We should have left a little earlier, but..."

Tabor was hovering by, waiting. Willis said quickly: "Have you two met? John Carrierco, my friend and client Mr. Tabor. Carrierco is head of the Transport Loaders' Union."

There was an instinct there, an infallible instinct. Carrierco did not put out his band but inclined his head instead and said courteously: "Sir."

Tabor said heartily: "Glad to know you, Carrierco." In the same breath, not conscious of the incongruity, he said: "I hope you've got a gun."

Bradley shuffled his feet and frowned and said: "Yes, he's got a gun, haven't you?"

Carrierco sighed. "Yes, I have a pistol. If you want to make trouble, Mr. Bradley... I suppose I ought to surrender it to you like a gentleman."

Bradley was glad of the recognition of his authority. He waved a helpless hand and said: "Under any other circumstances, of course... But for the moment... How did you get here?"

"We had to walk. Or rather, we ran, and for the Chief that is not easy. Someone came and told us that the *watu* were approaching, and so... I assure you, running for ten miles is neither easy nor dignified. We hid out in the bush close to the village for a while, and then we came here. It took us a long time. The Chief wanted to go back and fight these people by himself..."

"There are thirty or forty of them out there," Willis said.

Carrierco shrugged his shoulders elegantly. "More, Mr. Willis. Between the village and the valley and the coastline, there are more than a hundred of them. My informant said three groups of thirty or forty each." Carrierco, at heart politically minded, did not add that his union, seven thousand strong, paid two shillings each, on his secret orders, to the *Watu* arms fund.

Tabor said: "A hundred! Are you sure? That many?"

"They killed Chief M'Butu's brother last night, Mr. Willis. They cut off both his arms at the shoulders and left him there in the desert to die. But he reached the village and warned the Chief that they were coming for him too, and then he died. But still the Chief did not want to leave his people. If I had not insisted... You know Chief M'Butu. He did not become a chief through fear, of anything. He wanted to stay and rouse his people against the *watu*, but what chance would he have had? Openly, they had come to his village to kill him, and we were lucky that one of his wives, who was out looking for a lost goat, saw them in time. Many of the villagers must have seen them too, but there was nobody who would warn us except a frail old woman." He looked at Bradley reproachfully and said: "You see, Mr. Bradley, they do not believe anymore that their chief is a better man than they are, a man to be respected, a man to be protected; they have acquired your instincts for democracy. You have succeeded well in teaching them the basic principles of your ideas on equality; for a long time now, the Chief has been no longer a chief, but merely a man like any other, because this is what your Government has taught them."

"Let's forget the politics," Willis said. "I want to know where you propose to go from here? Because that's where we might have to go too."

Again, that elegant shrug. It seemed as if the question were trifling because the effort had been unavailing.

"We hoped to find a passing fisherman... But only one 'ngalau passed by this place all evening, and when we called him...he just paddled further out to sea."

"I see." Willis kicked at the dust for a moment, frowning, and said: "Seems simple enough then. We'll stay here all night and in the morning I'll take the Land Rover and go for help. There are enough guns to hold this place if they try anything. Can't imagine they will, anymore. A bus out in the open, surprise, that's one thing. But they know we're not just going to sit here and wait to get killed."

Carrierco did not answer, and Willis said sharply: "Well, don't you agree?"

Carrierco said smoothly: "Yes, of course, Mr. Willis. Of course. How many guns do we have? Mine is only...just a Luger, I'm afraid."

"Three rifles, two shotguns, a Luger. That should be enough."

Tabor said: "A couple of us on guard all night, there's no problem." He sighed. "I'll never understand these Africans if I live here for a hundred years. Carrierco's right... Hell, what's a hundred of them doing, letting us get to safety like this? They're not trying very hard, are they?" He looked up at the outline of the house and said: "Well, if this place is as strong as it looks, we could hold it against an army. What is it, anyway?"

"It's called Darhuzuni," Willis said. "Used to be a slavers' post, but now... now, it's nothing but a pile of stones."

They began to unload the stores from the Land-Rover.

Willis picked up the water can that was strapped on the back, shook it, frowning, then looked at the two spare cans that Adoula was lifting off. He turned to Babajee and said, worried: "How much water have you on your bus, Baba?"

The Indian looked at him blankly. "I think...I don't know, really..."

"Well, we'd better have a look."

Marion said: "We used most of ours on the radiator. That bus is quite a weight behind us."

Knowing the truth, shrinking from it, Babajee did not want to say anything, but as Willis climbed aboard the bus and began to look around, he came over and said hurriedly: "We would have filled up in Mwadi, but we didn't get there, and so..."

A search turned up two half-full water bags. The big tank under the chassis was dry as a bone.

Marion said lightly: "Then we'll have to manage with what we've got, won't we? We're not going to be here long, anyway." She looked at Willis in the silence and repeated: "Are we?"

There was just the slightest hesitation. "No. Of course we're not. Just overnight. First thing in the morning, we'll all be out of here. And we can get water from the old well before we leave, unless it's dry."

There was a short argument among the Africans. Chief M'Butu spoke with them for a while, and they heard him saying, insisting: "You will be safe here. The white men have rifles, they will protect you."

The passengers heard him out, and then one of them, whose name was Livingstone, said slowly: "You may be right, old man. But if we enter this house, we will have chosen sides. We will go back instead to our villages, on foot, and pray that the *watu* will let us pass."

"The *Bwana* District Officer said they killed one of your friends, that they cut off his head with a *panga*. He said they killed three others too, with their rifles. Stay with us, you will be safe."

They kept a stubborn silence, and their women waited, knowing that they would do what the men wanted them to do.

M'Butu said at last, turning away from them: "Do what you will, I will say no more."

Livingstone was a young man, a man from the town, and he did not want to be told what to do by an old chief whose authority was recognized no longer. He looked at the young boy who was with Adoula and said sharply: "And you, child? Will you grow up with

91

your own people, or with the white men?"

Mtoto looked unhappily at Adoula and said: "I will do what you will do."

Livingstone pointed a finger at Adoula and said accusingly: "I know you, Adoula. Do not keep this boy from his own people."

Adoula turned away and said nothing, and Mtoto went to join the others, and in a little while they were gone.

M'Butu went into the hall of the big house, where the sky was showing brightly through a hole in the roof, and said to Willis: "The passengers from the bus, they will not stay with us. They have gone back to their village."

Willis shrugged. "They might make it. I doubt it. They'd have been better off with us."

M'Butu said: "And this is what I told them, but..." He began to climb the broken stairway slowly.

In only a few moments M'Butu came back. He had reconnoitered the old house.

He was a huge man, powerful in spite of his age, and his belly hung down in folds over the robe he wore tightly around his enormous waist. When he talked, he moved his gigantic hands like the limbs of a ballet dancer. His sandal-shod feet were splayed, the toes gnarled and stubby, like the knots of a mangrove root in the swamps.

He raised a didactic finger and said, pointing up to the roof: "We must stay in this house, and one of us must watch from up there. Before you came, there were just the two of us, and I said to the man Carrierco: 'We can hold this fortress until the British come to rescue us...' And now that you are here, we are strong, too strong for any number of them. A gun on each side of the house...it is all we will need, with the others, who may sleep, in support when they are wanted."

He spoke like a general, and Willis looked at him curiously and said: "I believe you're enjoying all this."

The old man shook his head, his flabby cheeks dangling, and he chuckled. "Once there was a time when a chief was a leader of his people. If he could not lead them in their battles, he was no longer a chief. Once, it was like this in your own country too. We are not so different from you; if you take your mind back into the history you learned when you were young, I think you will find that your people then were as my people are today."

"The difference is in the change. Slower, or faster, that's all it is. We're both old men, M'Butu, and I'm closer to you than I am to young Bradley, and he's closer to Carrierco than he is to either of us. The old and the new. And if we stopped to think about it, we'd know that that's what we're fighting for, you and I; the status quo. Or rather, what the status quo used to be before the politicians started fart-arsing around with it."

M'Butu nodded slowly, his eyes amused. He said: "Yes, it was the politicians. The politicians and the businessmen. Once, our African society had its base in the home, in the family and in the tribe, which was an expansion of the family. But then, when you built your towns, the young men began to leave us, to make money which they did not need, to make money when they would have been better employed herding the tribal cattle. They found new friends who were not from their own tribe, friends with ideas just as deeply rooted as their own, but which were different, and it confused them. It destroyed the rigid authority of the tribe, and turned our young men into wastrels, because they began to learn things that even their fathers did not know. The young men became lost goats, wandering, unsure of their new knowledge, and restless."

They sat in silence for a while, squatting in a corner of bright moonlight under one of the windows. Willis said at last, thinking of the *watu* out there: "I think we're worrying for nothing. I just don't believe that there can be any danger *here*, not behind walls like these."

"You know the history of this unhappy house. It has always been dangerous here. There is a spirit in every old, abandoned house; and the spirit in Darhuzuni is the spirit of Death."

"And yet, you came here for shelter."

M'Butu shrugged. "We ran until we could run no more, and there was Darhuzuni, beckoning to us. I would not have chosen it, but..." He hit the wall with the flat of his huge hand and said: "The builders have gone, and the house is falling down. Is this the story of my land? Is this to be our fate too?"

A cloud crossed the moon, and the shadow brought with it a

breath of sudden cold. Willis said slowly: "Carrierco...I wouldn't have thought he'd be a friend of yours."

M'Butu grimaced. "No friend. He came here from Tanganyika for one reason only. In Tanganyika he found that the people were too gentle for him, too kind and tolerant to listen to the wickedness he preaches. He is a fine *msemaji*, a great orator, did you know that? And here, in Kenya, there is more fertile soil for the evil he sows."

"But he still came to warn you? There's a rumor, among some of the Europeans, that Carrierco is tied up with the *watu*. What do you think about that?"

"He was, for a while. Perhaps he would still like to be—under his own conditions. A leader no longer needs strength and bravery; in the twisted climate of political cunning which your new methods have brought to us, a leader needs a kind of insidious chicanery, the cunning of the leopard that will kill because it hates... Carrierco is a powerful politician, and he knows that oratory is not enough to control his semi-civilized workers; he knows that he also needs a strong force of terrorists to do his bidding, if only to keep his own men in line. But the *watu*...I do not think they want to be ruled by men like Carrierco, who seeks only his own aggrandizement. Carrierco is fighting for himself; the *watu* are fighting for a cause. However vile it is, they still believe it is a cause."

"And yet, Carrierco sides with you against them? I find it surprising."

"Because you know only Carrierco the politician, who makes inflammatory speeches and rouses his people against yours. You do not know Carrierco the man, the opportunist who will let nothing stand in his way. Carrierco the man is as much a savage under his European clothes as any of the *watu* out there. His wife is my granddaughter. I know. My daughter, too, once shared his house, and she tells me..."

He fell silent for a while, moodily trying to cross a great gulf. He said at last, heavily: "They lived on a farm, ten days' walk from here, she does not see him very often. And, when Carrierco left the farm four years ago and went to the town to preach his foolishness, he put on a European suit and dark glasses, and he learned to use a typewriter and to drive a car... He left the farm carrying his brown

94

shoes in his hand so that he would not spoil them, and the wife he left behind...he had her circumcised."

Again, the silence. Willis said, frowning: "It's common enough. A lot of them still do that."

"Not if they drive cars and use typewriters. And not in my tribe, nor in his."

"And that means?"

"It means that the new shape of life which Carrierco embraces is only on the surface. He does not believe in the modern ways he tells his people of. And, you must remember, that if a man does the things Carrierco does for other reasons than the ones he professes, then the true reasons are hidden only because they are evil. I learned many years ago to judge a man not by what he *does*, but by what he *thinks*. And so, I tell you, Carrierco lives like a white man, and yet he infibulates his wife like a savage, and this can only mean that there is a *pepo*, a spirit of evil inside him. Inside him, it is the old order he cherishes, not the new one that he pretends to follow. You have taught him enough of your ways, and now he wants to turn that learning to his own benefit; and since he is a man of cunning but no stature, he can only do this if the people around him are more simple than he is. The old order of ignorance, held in place by the thin layer of civilization that Carrierco represents."

"But now, his life is at stake, not his philosophy."

"And we will remember that he is not what he appears to be."

"You think he might try and go over to them?"

"Only if," M'Butu said, "only if he believes that we cannot survive. When Carrierco leaves us, we will know that the odds against us have become too strong."

But it was not Carrierco who left Darhuzuni that night. Later, when the sleep was heavy about them and the first light was showing in the sky, Babajee came running in excitedly and said: "Adoula, he's gone!"

Willis got quickly to his feet. "Adoula? Surely not..."

"I saw him, Mr. Willis. I tried to stop him. He went out the front door and ran towards the rocks over there. He was...I think he was crying."

Tabor was not sure whether it was anger or sorrow he saw on Willis' taut face. He said: "How long's he been with you?"

Willis looked away from him. "Twelve years. All through the Mau Man... They tried to kill him then because he wouldn't take the Oath. He was one of the few who stuck by us. It's hard...hard to believe."

"Maybe...maybe there's some other explanation."

All the old loyalties were collapsing around him. It was the same old story all over again: *Trust no one. Your friend is your enemy. Your servant is your executioner.* The load of his thoughts was hard to bear. Willis said sadly: "No. It's just an indication...how strong they really are. The same old story. We never know how big the gulf is until we try to look across it." He looked at Tabor and said: "You never want to accept the obvious, do you?"

"No. Not if I don't like the looks of it."

"I envy you. I would dearly like to think that Adoula has gone for help."

"Maybe he has."

"Without a word to me? I'm like a father to him." His voice heavy with pain, Willis said: "However much we try, we'll never understand what goes inside their heads. I cannot, *will* not believe he's gone to join them, and yet... I know how close it got with the Mau Mau, how tightly his loyalty was stretched then. And now..." There was an infinite loneliness in his voice. "Now, I wish to God I could make myself believe what I *want* to believe. But I can't."

"One thing we can be glad of," Tabor said. Willis, silent, looked at him. Tabor said: "If he's going to fight with them against us, he just threw away a great opportunity. He could have killed us both before he left. I wonder why he didn't try."

And this was the first question Adoula was asked when he came to the great pile of jagged boulders where the tiny fire had been lit. A dozen strong hands came out of the pitch black night and grabbed him and threw him to the ground, and someone's foot pressed his face into the sand, and he heard a voice growl: "Did you kill any of them before you left, boy?"

Adoula spluttered: "No, I did not. I came to tell you...there are too many of them, they are too strong."

"How many guns,

He twisted his face around and saw only the khaki shorts and the strong, thick-muscled legs. He said: "Let me get up, and I will tell you."

The man with the thick legs, who seemed to be their leader, grunted an order, and Adoula was pulled roughly to his feet. He was shocked to see them in the firelight; their bodies were painted like the old-time warriors his grandfather had told him about, and many of them were strangers, from tribes he could not even recognize, with harsh scars down their cheeks; some of them even had their teeth filed, and he thought with sudden revulsion: *The white men think that these are my people...*

He was not afraid of them. He said: "I came to tell you that they are well armed. If you try to kill them, there will be much bloodshed. It is better you let them go."

The leader stared at him for a moment, then took off his army cap and hit him across the face with it. Adoula felt the blood stream down his chin and realized that there were razor blades stitched to the cap's visor.

He brushed at the blood and said, stubbornly: "It is no good to be angry. Better you go away."

The leader said again: "How many guns?"

"The two white men, the hunters, are well armed, and so is the white woman. The *Bwana* District Officer has a rifle too, and the African Carrierco has a pistol."

The leader scoffed at him: "Five guns, and we are an army. You still want us to go away?"

Adoula said steadily: "It would be better."

"They sent you here to tell me this?"

"No. I came because I wanted to come."

"And you will fight with us against them?"

"No. I will not fight for you against them, and I will not fight for them against you."

"You're either for us or against us, boy."

97

"No. I will not fight. They would have given me a gun if I had asked for it."

"They trust you."

"They trust me."

"The white men."

"My master trusts me."

A small figure approached him in the darkness and said hesitantly: "Adoula? Why did you come?"

It was the child Mtoto. Adoula looked at him and saw the fright in his eyes, and then the thick-set man laughed and said: "Mtoto, you see what we have saved you from? You would grow up to be like this, a servant to the white man. Now, go and fetch wood for the fire."

As Mtoto, not meeting Adoula's eyes, hesitated, the leader said sharply: "Go! And there is nothing to be afraid of, you are with your own people." He turned back to Adoula and said: "If you want to go back and steal their guns..."

"No. I will not fight against my master."

The leader grinned, an evil, savage grin, with no humor in it. Then he stretched out his open hand and one of the others put a *panga* in it, and as two of the warriors held his arms, Adoula saw the blade go slowly up and then back, high above the stocky man's head.

When it flashed down, it sliced through Adoula neatly, efficiently, down from the shoulder as far as the waist. The warriors laughed and slung the body around to fall to the thirsty sand, and they went back to the fire and began to smoke their cigarettes.

One of the two African women from the bus, the younger of the two, who had already been raped eleven times, lay sobbing beside them. The leader came over and kicked her in the side, and said roughly: "Stop your weeping and come with me."

Silently, she got up and followed him into the bushes.

CHAPTER 7

Over the old stone house the night hung heavy.

And in the darkness below, with whispering and the scuttling of bare feet in the sand, the *watu* were gathering, staring in silence up at the high, crumbling walls, wondering how close they dared approach, looking at the moving shadows that were peering down on them too, watching, gauging the strength of the shadowy forces that were slowly coming together in a clash that would be filled with terror and with pent-up evil.

"A siege?" It did not seem possible. Secure in the custom of the past, Willis said with contempt: "They'll never dare attack us. We'll take it in turns to keep watch, let them see we're not sleeping, that's all we have to do."

They piled the stores from the truck in the central hall, ate in silence from the cans of corned beef, posted their first sentries, and turned in for restless sleep, wrapped up in blankets against the cold night air.

Only the night sounds of the bush came to them. The distant sound of a bird, and then silence. The moan of a prowling lion, and then silence; the madwoman shriek of a hunting hyena, and then again...silence.

Through the battered embrasure of the window, the moon had gone down over the sea, far below them, and it seemed as if the sea itself had turned into a limitless sheet of glass, motionless, unsurfed and silent; it was so quiet when Tabor awoke that he found himself straining his ears to hear the sound of the lizard's tongue as it flicked out to trap a sleeping fly.

He rubbed the sleep out of his red-rimmed eyes and grimaced in the semidarkness, watching the flickering light of the candle in the corner. His voice was a whisper: "If they had a general, they would rush us."

Beside him, Willis stirred, half asleep, and sat up to peer at the dial of his watch, twisting his wrist so that it might catch the yellow light. He said sleepily: "Half past two. And there's the story of Africa in a nutshell. Plenty of people to do things and no one to tell them what to do." He was suddenly wide awake, as though the danger had been forgotten for a while and then suddenly remembered. He said briskly: "They've been dependent on us for too long now, and when they're fighting the white man there's no longer a white man to turn to for the help they've always wanted. That's why, in the long run, a rising like this is bound to fizzle out."

Were the experts always right? The problem had been going on for a long time. As the sleep went away, the clarity came; Tabor snorted, a grunt of disbelief. He said: "You've been too close to it all. The long view."

"It's only a question of time," Willis insisted. "In time, they all fizzle out."

"It might just be a hell of a long time, at that."

"Maybe. There've always been lion men, and leopard men, and wildebeest men... One cult dies, another is born. It's nothing new."

"It's new because they're getting aware of the world around them. Maybe if you British had taught them a little more..."

"Or a little less..."

"The Mau Mau should have shown you what can happen when a cult turns political."

There was suddenly a savagery in Willis' voice: "The Mau Mau was nothing but terrorism. Nothing else."

"So was the French Revolution, at first. But it changed the course of history for half the world."

Willis sighed patiently. The more detached, the more remote the view, the simpler it all seemed. Could a man cross half the world and see more clearly through the fog that had obscured the issues for nearly a century?

He said mildly: "Don't try to dignify a terrorist outbreak like this by calling it a revolution. It's the Leopard Men all over, that's all."

Unaware, Tabor said: "Or the Mau Mau." He could not know how deeply the phrase cut, deep to the bone in anguish that Willis had never forgotten, that was never far from his thoughts and that came back, when he least expected it, in painful spasms. Tabor said flatly (but worrying about the sadness there): "If they ever get together, these people, it will be through one of the cults, as you call them, and a catalyst...some smart politician to make use of them is all it needs. The Mau Mau failed because it was tribal, you must know that. If they'd got together with the Masai, or the Wagogo..."

Willis snorted scornfully. "And if you'd been out here a few years longer you'd know that's impossible. The Kikuyu tribe is an entity, the Nandi is an entity, the Masai is an entity... There's not a single tribe that doesn't regard its neighbor as a mortal enemy..."

"But if they ever get together..."

"They never will."

"They're beginning to."

"Never! Why is it that Americans always think of revolt in terms of the Civil War? It's not as simple as all that! You think that because your Southern States united, the African tribes will too, but take my word for it, they never will. In the South you had a common heritage, something to keep the people together... But these people, their heritages are separate and all founded on mutual distrust and hatred, every one of them...and that's the essential difference." He said wearily: "You think an African farmer's like a Kentucky farmer because they both work the soil? The only thing we failed to teach them is that the world is getting smaller and they just have to conform to our ways."

Tabor did not want to argue. He said ruefully: "Or we to theirs. After all, this is their country."

Willis turned to him in astonishment: "Whose country?"

"Well, the blacks..."

The temper was beginning to mount; it was an argument he had heard too often before. Willis said angrily: "You know how many whites were born out here? And what the hell do you mean when you say the blacks anyway? You mean the Swahili tribes? Or the Hottentots, or the Zulus, or the Somalis, or the Bantu? How far back do you want to go? We took this country from the Germans, who had taken it from the Portuguese, who had taken it from the Arabs. Before that... Hell, nobody knows what nomadic were wandering about here, fighting each other for it, nor how long they stayed. So, who has proper claim to it? Isn't there more right for those who worked the land, who turned it from swamp and desert into the fine farms we have today? And believe me, that wasn't easy! *We* cleared it, *we* drained it, *we* fertilized it, *we* made the land what it is today... And *we* suffered with it." He broke off sharply, aware that Tabor was watching him closely. He said sullenly: "We built something here worth having, and they tried to take it from us."

Tabor said curiously: "I spoke of the Mau Man once before, and you raised hell then, too. Kind of sets you off, doesn't it?"

Willis shook his head and said nothing. A cold breeze came through the window and the candle flickered. A rat scuttled across the torn canvas that had once been a tightly stretched ceiling under the heavy rafters.

Willis said at last, sighing: "And it's time to relieve Marion."

"Half an hour to go." Tabor thought for a while, wondering about her, and at last said curiously: "A country full of kooks... There's something strange that drives that woman. I wish I knew what it was."

There was a touch of bitterness in Willis' voice, a touch of despair. "Hatred."

"Hatred? I don't believe it! Everything you could call the antithesis of hatred...she's got it."

"Hatred of herself."

It was eerie, talking quietly in the candlelight, as though they were living in another era, where even the emotions were primitive and undeveloped. And Marion, was she really up on the roof there, watching silently in the darkness? Or was she within earshot, hearing their whispered comments about her? He found it hard not to peer into the corners to search for her.

Willis said slowly: "You heard the stories, you must have heard them."

"Gossip, I never listen to it."

"Most of it came from her herself. What she did that night... It's been nibbling at her ever since, eating at her, consuming her, gnawing her down to the marrow. And she knows the pain of it. Sometimes, if you can watch her unawares..."

"It's mighty hard to do that too."

"Yes, I know. There's a barrier she's built up. You can't get through it. Nobody can. One day the barrier will break, and there'll be a flood, and when it's gone down there'll be a new Marion there that you and I have never known. I wish to God it *would* break, I wish to God I could see her unprotected, unsure, dependent, dependent on something other than the hardness of that shell she's built. Maybe the shell protects her; but it's destroying her, too, and if I had one last wish in this world... I'd want to break through it and find the woman underneath..."

There was a question Tabor had long been wanting to ask. He said uncomfortably, but glad of his friendship with Willis, glad it was strong enough to permit of a discussion like this: "Somehow, the fact that it's none of my damn business... But...has it ever occurred to you that the whole thing might be a lie? From beginning to end?"

"I wish it were. I wish to God it were."

"There might be a reason tucked away some place, a reason for her to lie about it, a reason we can't even guess at."

"No," Willis said morosely. "Not a chance. She drove up to her house that night, and she found her husband dead drunk on the sofa, and she took the poker from the fireplace, and she killed him with it."

"And, from all accounts, he deserved it."

"You knew Cassel just well enough to realize what a bastard he really turned out to be, but that doesn't justify it. And worse...she boasts about it."

Tabor said hopelessly: "He was such a... If only she'd just divorced him!"

Willis got to his feet, stripped off his clothes, and rubbed at his body with a dry towel. He said clearly: "The facts are there. Bradley was the District Officer in charge of the case. Once he damn near had her arrested, but she said quite simply: 'I'll deny everything in court. Everything!' And what she chooses to say in a cocktail bar is hardly evidence. The houseboy said that Cassel was dead when she got home... She'd have been acquitted in five minutes for lack of evidence. So, rather than have her enjoy the security of double jeopardy, they simply closed the case. Unsolved."

He clapped Tabor on the back, slipped into his clothes and went up on the roof to relieve Marion.

She had moved from the high point by the old chimney and was precariously perched on the overhang above the broken tower that had once been a Portuguese lookout. She whistled gently in the darkness when she heard him coming, and he slithered over the loose clay tiles to go to her.

He tested the stonework with his shoulder, pushing it gently and feeling the slightest movement where the old mortar came away. He said cheerfully: "I hope you realize this lot's liable to come down if you as much as look it."

She shook her hair back from her face in a gesture that was somehow childlike and said: "I know. But there's a wider field of view here. One of them tried to get at the Land Rover."

"Oh?" There was sudden alarm there. "You should have called out."

She shook her head again, and a finger strayed to the long hair. She looked very fragile against the stonework.

"Half an hour ago. I was getting ready for a careful shot, but it was too dark, he was just a shadow. But he heard me moving and beat it. They haven't tried again."

"I wish I knew how many of them are out there. I don't believe they're as strong as Carrierco thinks."

She said anxiously: "However many there are...you're not going to make a run for it?"

"I don't know. I've been thinking about it. Chances are there's not a good shot among them, and maybe in the truck I could make a fast enough getaway. I just don't know."

"Don't try it," she urged. "If we lose you..."

"Or my rifle. Might be better to wait as long as we can. In a day, two at the most, they'll probably give up. If not... Let's play it off the cuff."

"There's bound to be someone along sooner or later."

"We could stay here for a year and not be found. No one ever comes this way."

"Wait a day or two. We can hold out for a week if necessary."

"We'll see." He was worried about the water. She asked: "Are the others still asleep?"

"Yes. Did Bradley have anything to report when you took over?"

"Nothing." The lines at her mouth tightened. "You know I'm not very fond of Bradley, but...he was half asleep when I relieved him."

The shock of his sudden anger was like a blow. Could a man sleep with so much to fear out there in the night? Could a man be such a fool as to think he was safe from those he had always loved, even when that love was not returned, but came back rather as a hatred of his condescension? Was his misunderstanding of their savagery so remote that he really could not believe their knives were sharp and the evil in them acute? Had the first fear gone so far away?

She saw the dismay on his face and said quickly: "Dozing, not really asleep. But you could hardly call it wide awake either. He didn't hear me coming, and God knows I made more noise than I should."

He waited, worrying about it in the stillness. Their voices were low, soft, more gentle than the night.

She said: "He said he'd heard me, but I'm damn sure he hadn't."

Willis raised a hopeless hand. "They could have killed us all."

"No. If they'd got into the building I'd have heard them, asleep or not. So would you, so would M'Butu. And so would Tabor."

"They move like cats."

"I know. But fear's a mighty good waker-upper, and I'm scared, I don't mind admitting it." She said impatiently: "Why haven't they rushed us, can you tell me that?"

"They know how many guns we have. And even a determined rush, even in the night..."

"And now the night is going."

He touched her arm, feeling the cold there. "Go to sleep, another two hours to daylight. We just might need you then."

"Carrierco's over on the other side. He thinks a fisherman or two might go by on the early tide. We saw some flares out on the water an hour ago."

"Yes, they're burning old tires, I could smell the rubber. But they were a long way off."

"Too far to be useful even if they wanted to."

"The *watu* have been in their village. It's not likely they'll be of any help to us. By daylight there won't be a fisherman in sight."

She stood up and balanced herself precariously on the edge of the overhang, stretching her legs; he could almost hear the cramped muscles moving in the silence, and the wind was cold around them.

She said angrily: "There must be someone in the village who's against them! The Chief's men..."

"The Chief is alone, absolutely alone. That's why they want to kill him, he's the only holdout. With him gone...there's not a warrior among them who will dare to take sides against the *watu*. They won't fight with them, maybe, but they won't fight against them either."

All that he loved was fast disappearing, lost in a new world where there was only hatred and confusion. He said bitterly: "Someone's got at them. No, they won't move a finger to help us."

"But it's a hope."

"There's always hope. Go and sleep."

The sun came up fast on an empty desert, driving away the cold moisture of the night, and in less than an hour the earth was parched again.

Tabor stood on the top of the portico, staring down at the stubby square of the truck, his face dark with anger. He turned away and clambered up the stairs towards the roof.

Willis turned to see him coming and said: "Yes, I know, I've seen it."

Tabor was furious. "How the hell?... How the bloody hell?"

"The night was as black as a cat. Someone crept up and sawed through the tires with a *panga*."

"With someone watching it all night? I want to know who it was, Willis. You realize that's our only way of getting out of here?"

106

His voice was harsh with anger. Glaring down at the well, he said: "That damned well... M'Butu thinks there might be water a few feet down. We'd better find out, fast." He looked at the truck again and swore. "Our only way out of here, how in hell...!"

Willis refused to let his exasperation show. He said, worried and trying to keep an even temper: "Marion said she saw a shadow move there but scared it away. Before that..."

"Bradley!"

"It was dark, so dark there could have been a dozen of them around it."

"He's got ears, hasn't he?"

"Can you hear a lion move in the night?"

"That bastard! In a fix like this, Bradley's a goddam liability."

"We don't know it happened when he was on guard, not for sure. It could have been while I was here too. Easily."

Tabor hesitated. "I'll bet." He growled. "A chain snaps, it's always at the weakest link."

"But we can't blame him unless we're sure. And we're not sure."

Tabor said: "I am."

Willis said sharply: "Don't take it out on him! It could easily have been me."

"If you believe that..."

"No, I don't really. But, unless we're certain..."

"All right, all right." He looked down at the Land Rover again, flat on its tires, and said: "That bastard!" He turned to Willis and frowned, and said: "How far to walk if we decide that's the best thing to do?"

"Too far. They might just fade away into the desert, they probably will, but...even so, we'll never know they're not still out there, hiding, waiting for us to leave the only protection within a hundred miles. Two women with us, remember."

"Anyone liable to find out about us here? The police? What about Bradley's office? They must know where he went."

"He was out on safari. If they don't hear from him in a couple of weeks, maybe they'll begin to scout around."

Tabor said wrathfully: "You mean to say a bunch of bloody

savages can rampage around the desert, killing everything in sight, and no one's going to know about it?"

"That's exactly what I mean," Willis said patiently. "We're a long way from civilization here."

"And right on the edge of the sea. There must be a boat somewhere..."

"Nothing. And nothing liable to sail by, either."

Tabor looked at the broken rafters and said, jerking his head towards them: "We've got a raft there if we try hard enough."

"I thought about that, too. There's the problem of getting it down to the water. It's three hundred feet and more."

"How much rope have we got?"

"Not enough. Not nearly enough. And we'd need what we have to lash the spars together. There's another point to bear in mind; *if* we can make a raft, *if* we can get it down into the water, *if* we can get it away from the shore, once we leave the fort they'll come pouring over the walls... They'll be above us firing down. I don't care how bad their shooting is, in the time it takes us to get out of range, someone's going to get killed, if not all of us."

Well, let's face that problem when we get to it."

"You don't give up easily, do you?"

"Like hell. I want to be sure we can hold if we have to, and I want to be sure we can get out if we have to, it's as simple as that. We'll make a raft."

"All right. Three of us on guard, the rest at work. It'll give us something to do besides worry."

When they clambered down and told Marion about the slashed tires on the truck, her blue eyes were hard.

"Not while I was up there," she said with certainty.

Willis sighed. "A night sound in the bush is all that would have been heard. And it was black, black, black out there."

She looked at Bradley, white-faced and angry, and said nothing, holding his look, sitting up on the cold stone floor with her blanket draped across her knees and running a hand through her hair. She said accusingly: "I didn't believe you were as wide awake as you should have been."

Bradly said angrily: "I would have heard them... It must have been...it wasn't while I was there."

Marion's eyes were hard. "Then you think it was me?"

"No, I just..."

"Or Willis, after I'd gone?"

Willis said patiently: "It's a thing we'll never know, so why don't we drop it? While *someone* was on watch, they crept up and slashed the tires. I don't care who the hell it was, it's done and that's all there is to it."

She looked at Bradley and said coldly: "They could have got in and killed us all."

Bradley blinked at her, his lips tight, and said nothing, then turned and went quickly out of the room. His shoulders were hunched and he was trembling.

Marion threw aside the blanket and stretched her long, slim arms. In the early light the flesh at the edges of her breast was white, showing up the dark brown of her shoulders,

Willis said good-humoredly, driving away her anger: "How you can look good at this hour of the morning..."

She managed a laugh. "I might look a little better if I could rinse some of this dirt off... How much water do we have?"

"Counting all the water bottles, what's left of them, counting M'Butu's goatskin, we've got a total of just over half a gallon. But we should be able to clean out the well."

"I hope so. Any liquor?"

"A full bottle of gin, about a third of a bottle of whiskey, but that's no good if we're thirsty."

"Ten pints and nine people," Tabor said.

Willis said: "Half a cup a day each, starting when we really begin to need it. That gives us...four days before we're uncomfortably thirsty, a week before there's any real danger."

Tabor said dispassionately: "We're not going to be here for a week, not if I can help it."

Willis said: "And the chances are they'll try and pin us down for a couple of days, and then we'll suddenly find they've all gone."

Marion's face was grave. "And then?"

Willis went to the window and leaned into the embrasure, staring out across the sea.

"It's a good question. Tabor's right, let's look at the worst that can happen. Let's assume we're as badly off as we might be. If we start walking out, we're liable to find them waiting for us when we're well clear of these protecting walls. Let's not assume that they're all idiots. And without a wall around us, on foot... The nearest help is a damn long way away, on foot."

Marion said calmly: "Sixty miles. And with how much water left? It's a problem, isn't it?"

Tabor said sourly: "Are we going to argue all day? We clean out the well and we build a raft, so let's start working."

Marion turned to him with a sort of desperation in her voice: "This is the twentieth century, for God's sake! Eight of us holed up with a crowd of bloody savages out there... It doesn't make sense."

Willis turned back from the window and said slowly: "Only it's not the twentieth century anymore. The twentieth century is out there somewhere, a long way across that water. This is Africa, and we are back in the Middle Ages." He added lightly: "But in a few days' time we'll be joking about this over a bottle of champagne in the Norfolk Hotel." He looked down at her as she sat there, with her arms around her knees, her long hair falling down over her bare shoulders. "We'll be out of here pretty soon, as you must know. You've got more horse sense than any of us."

She threw aside the blanket with a quick motion of her wrist and stood up, wiggling her toes. "If that's supposed to be a compliment... Now, get the hell out of my bedroom and let me get dressed."

Without waiting for them to move, she began to unfasten her brassiere, and when they stood looking at her, marveling at her slim beauty, she said again: "Go on, go and find M'Butu. I want to rub myself down."

The old chief had wedged his great bulk securely between the eroded chimney stacks, and they could only reach him by crawling hazardously across the exposed rafters and over the dusty tie beams.

Willis said incredulously: "How the devil did you manage to get up here?"

He pulled the binoculars from their case and tested one of the iron tie rods that held the old walls together before balancing himself precariously against it and swinging himself up onto the tiles.

The sea was dangerously far below, the surf beginning to move now, very gently, against the rocks; soon, it would be pounding them mercilessly, as it had pounded them since the beginnings of history, pounding hopelessly over a million empty years.

M'Butu was pointing out into the desert. He swung his arm around and said gravely: "There, and there, and there. My eyes are getting old, but I would say more than fifty of them. Many of them have rifles, very many."

Willis steadied the binoculars. "Hell, I can't even see them with the glasses."

"By the thorn trees, where the rocks are. Eight of them. Four more under the mimosa, ten or twelve behind the big rock that looks like a lion's head."

The eight were not very far away. When Willis got them in focus, he saw that they were squatting, very still, half hidden by shrubbery and by the boulders that were dotted there; two of them were peering straight at him, squinting their eyes, and as he watched, they exchanged a silent word and then ducked quickly out of sight. He knew that they were scared by the binoculars.

He said gruffly: "Bushmen. The evil eye." He put away the glasses and said: "What about you, M'Butu? Are you afraid of the evil eye too?"

The old man thought for a while, and then his chubby breasts began to shake and his chins quivered as he began to laugh, silently, completely moved by some inner thoughts he wanted to voice. He said: "Of course not! I have learned better. But please do not look at me through the glasses, just the same. It is not wise to taunt the old gods, even when you are quite sure they do not exist."

"What are your gods, M'Butu?"

The Chief was suddenly grave again as he tried to shift his weight between the confining brickworks. Willis put down the leather case and sat beside him, wedging a foot hard in among the laths of the roof and testing their strength fearfully.

"My gods? They are Madu, who takes care of my crops, and

Kalufu, who brings the rain, and Sada-Sumu, who will burn my house down if I do not hang a piece of red string outside my door."

"And Jesus Christ?"

M'Butu shrugged. "A chief, like any other chief. Perhaps not a very good one. Perhaps Mohammed was a better chief. I do not know. At least, he converted half of Africa; more than the Christian missionaries did."

"Because he used the sword instead of the Book."

"Look out there into the desert and you will see that my people understand the sword better than the Book."

"The Christians have a more gentle way."

M'Butu said swiftly: "It was not always so. The history of your church has not always been gentle. And for the misguided simpletons your missionaries have been teaching, for them the harsher aspects are easier to accept, because these aspects are closer to their own inherent ways. They take from your Faith only what is bad; the good is too abstruse for them to understand."

M'Butu's eldest son had long ago gone to London to study, and when he came back, once in a few years, dressed in strange, uncomfortable white man's clothes that M'Butu regarded with tolerant good humor, but which offended most of the villagers, he would sit under the thorn tree in the village square (on a chair rather than on a stone, because now he was a civilized man), and talk to the fascinated warriors about the amazing things he had learned, tell them of the great, strange weaknesses in the white man's civilization that the white men had told him about in their school, strange because the warriors knew that there were no such weaknesses, that the white man was at one time their own strength and their master. He had brought back some photographs, too, taken with a camera which the Friends of Africa had given him, and one of them showed him standing in Trafalgar Square, proud and erect in his new English clothes, one foot on a small green block, while a red-jacketed white man cleaned his shoes; it was a photograph at which the warriors stared in unbelieving wonder.

M'Butu said scornfully: "Look out there and you will see that we are hiding from savages who have learned a little of your faith; they have learned too much about it, perhaps, enough to question it, and they have learned that it is good only in parts. And a chief, a father, a priest...even a Faith, they must be good all the time, not merely for a few recent moments of history. And it is because there have always been parts of your faith that are bad that these poor people..." He hesitated and looked at Willis quizzically. "You do not question me when I say poor people?"

"No."

"They are poor because they are confused. Your differing missionaries teach them differing beliefs...what one says, the other denies. So they have chosen to believe only that which they can understand. And the drinking of blood is easy for them to understand because this, too, is part of the heritage of the tribal gods they once believed in. It is all very simple, really. And I believe too that the only people left who will believe what the missionaries say are the poor Africans. Am I not right?"

"Maybe."

"If you tell me that you believe what they preach, then I will believe you."

"No, I do not believe it. Not all of it."

"Then I will not believe it either. We have known each other for a long time, you and I, and I know that you cannot lie to me."

"I do not want to lie to you."

"Then tell me this." The old chief scratched at his enormous belly and said: "Tell me why you let your missionaries teach my people that you know to be wrong? That is the sickness that is taking my countrymen back into savagery. Among your people, the only believers left are the missionaries, and they all teach different things, each swearing that he is right. You yourselves no longer believe these things and yet you expect us to believe them, and wonder why we question the new Faith with which you want to replace the teachings of our ancestors. You teach our people about the gods you no longer believe in yourselves, but if you had taught them, instead, to build roads, to build ships, to build bridges... If you had taught them how to fight hunger instead of how to believe in yet another god who would give them some sort of mystical comfort... They already had enough of those mystical gods."

"You are wrong in one thing," Willis said. "We tried to teach them to build, we tried hard."

M'Butu, puzzled about this for a moment, said slowly: "Perhaps you did, I do not know. But if you tried, you did not succeed."

"And that's hardly our fault. We sent your sons to England to study, many of them. And what did they study? To be doctors, or lawyers, nothing else. To study to be an engineer, you know what that means... It presupposes physical work, and you well know what a stigma physical work is for your people."

M'Butu nodded sadly. "I know. To be fair, I used to tell them the same thing myself. 'Work,' I would tell them, 'is for women and animals only...'" He added mischievously: "And for white men, of course." Suddenly grave again, he said: "For the men of my tribe, fighting was always the only way of life, and there were women in plenty to toil. And if it was undignified for them to take a shovel in their hands... Yes, perhaps the fault is ours too. So we have many learned men who can argue; but not one who can build a road."

They sat there together, the two old men, and they thought about the old ways they had both once known.

Willis said abruptly: "They got at the truck during the night. We can't get away in it."

M'Butu's eyes were stolid and unmoved. He nodded his head slowly, the chins forming and reforming at his neck. "And the well?"

"We are going to try and clean it out today."

"If you have to ration the water, give mine to the white woman."

"We'll all share equally."

"I do not need water." He began to laugh again and patted his fat paunch happily. "Here, inside here, like a camel. There is water enough for seventeen days. But if you dig into the well... It is true." He put a pudgy finger first at his wrist, then at his elbow, then at his shoulder. "This much under the sand, or this much, or this much...there will be water. It was a good well once, sweet water, plenty of it. At the length of a man's arm under the sand, much less perhaps. But the entrance to it is narrow. I do not know if a man can get his body down there."

"Babajee, perhaps."

M'Butu nodded. "For a great number of years the Asian has

fattened himself on us. It is good that Babajee's fat has gone into the bank and not into his belly."

They startled as the rending sound of creaking wood came to them, and Willis said quickly: "It's Tabor. He wants to make a raft out of the roof timbers."

M'Butu nodded. "For *Bwana* Tabor, everything is simple! The sea is our friend, but the friend is so far away that he is of no help. And if we leave the protection of these walls... *Bwana* Tabor cannot see that we need patience, not rafts. For him it is too simple."

Willis said, smiling: "A tribal affliction of his people. But sometimes the simplest answer is the best one. Did you sleep at all?"

"With one eye only. First one eye, and then the other."

"Then you'd better get down from here and try to sleep for a while. It's Petna's turn to stand guard." He said hesitantly: "I'm assuming that they won't try to rush us. If they wanted to do that, I think they'd have come in the night. What do you think, am I right?"

M'Butu said: "Perhaps. But there is one thing you and I both know about my people; the one thing you have not been able to teach them—is to reason for themselves. If someone tells them to attack us, they will. If they are told to wait for us to die, they will do that too."

"Someone?" Willis looked at him suspiciously. "Is there something I ought to know about?"

For a long time M'Butu did not answer. Weighing his words carefully, not wanting events to prove his estimate wrong, he said at last: "Some of my own warriors are out there with them, some of my own tribesmen. And I must think what I myself would be doing if I were among them."

"And."

"I think I would be waiting for the witch doctor."

Willis grunted. "You want to come down and get some sleep?"

M'Butu shook his head. "Better I stay up here. Enough trouble getting *up*, more trouble getting *down*."

"Then try and sleep. Petna Babajee is coming up to relieve you."

"Better put her here close me. I like a young girl close to me."

"Don't try to take her mind off the watching."

"Tell her to shout if she is frightened, and to throw me the rifle.

Not to wait if I am asleep. By the time the rifle has left her hand I will be firing it."

"You should be ashamed of yourself, protected by a young girl."

M'Butu grinned happily and said: "The same lies with her." He gestured at his loins and said: "A young girl should hold this in her hand, not a rifle."

"You are a lecherous old bastard."

"I am a man." He looked at Willis slyly and said: "The lust has not left your loins, so why do you think it has left mine?"

Willis heard Petna trying to make the crossing and went over to help her, pulling her by brute force up onto the roof. She was trembling and he could see the weary anguish in her face.

He said gently: "It's going to be all right."

He wished for a moment that he were alone with her up here, just the two of them together, and he looked quickly across to M'Butu and saw that the old man had turned away his head. He put his arm around her and squeezed her narrow waist, knowing how much he loved her, but he could not drive away the trembling.

She said quietly: "Mr. Tabor told me about the truck. You don't believe it was Bradley's fault, do you?"

"No, not really."

"It was so dark... He does not hear very well."

"Don't worry about it. M'Butu will stay here with you, but he'll sleep."

He helped her across the tiles, reaching out for the rafters to steady himself, and when he had brought her to the chimney and given her the rifle, the old man had wrapped himself up in the blanket and had closed his eyes.

In a moment, he opened them again, looked at Petna, and said: "Fire one shot and throw me the rifle. Before the bullet leaves the barrel I will be ready and waiting for it."

She tucked the yellow sari tighter around her slim body and sat on her heels close by the chimney, staring out into the bush, the rifle incongruously held across her splendid breast.

Willis crouched down beside her and kissed her once, quickly, with an oblique glance at M'Butu, and whispered: "Don't worry, it's going to be all right. One way or the other, it's going to be all right."

She stared fearfully out into the hot desert, and he pointed and said: "Over by the boulders, mostly, but keep your eyes wide. It's more than three hundred yards, and even if they charge we'll have plenty of time. If they should cross the desert we'll stop them at the wall. If they cross the wall we'll stop them at the house. And if they get into the house they'll never be able to reach the roof. We're all good shots and there's nothing to worry about, all right?" She nodded, not looking at him. He put his hand gently on her breast and said: "I love you, my darling, and I'll never let them get near you. If anything moves you don't like the look of...you know what to do. And keep under cover."

He kissed her quickly again, and for a moment she clutched at him, fearfully. He gently disengaged her, groped his way back to the opening, swung himself down onto the stairway, and stood silent in the shade of the roof, remembering. *I love you too much to let them get near you...* The words had come to him unthinking, and now the memory of the last time brought its terrible pain down on him, unmuted by the passing of twelve long years.

CHAPTER 8

Twelve years ago. Had it really been so long?

Then, too, the pattern had been the same as it was now. There had been the same casual negligence, the inattention to a simple truth that had been so long accepted that it had become, by habit, relegated to the furthest recesses of the European mind, to be ignored and only remembered in time of sudden stress; the truth that the African was a dangerous child, whose insouciance could turn, in an instant, to fearful violence. The African had an ability to laugh at his worries that was childlike in the extreme, and you felt, watching his laughter, that he was a happy man who was inured to discontent and therefore harmless. But though the mind was childlike, the body was not; the body was tough, and impulsive, and dangerous, and the same white teeth that showed so easily in laughter could, when he was pushed too far, bite.

In those days, they had another name. They called themselves the Mau Mau, the Hidden People, because they too were children of the darkness, just like these.

Twelve years ago...

Up on the forested mountain, the air was cool, but he could feel the sweat soaking into the back of his khaki shirt, and he did not know how much of it was due to the exertion of the hasty run, and how much was fear.

The great camphor trees towered high above them, interspersed with yellowwood, and through a gap in the greenery he could see the giant bamboo high up on the furthermost slopes. The water dripped

118

from the branches into the sludge in which they lay, the thick black sludge that was the forest humus in which all living things struggled and fought for survival as he was struggling and fighting, too.

There was no break in the shooting. The Mau Mau were fresh from their raid on the arsenal in Nyeri, and were using .303 caliber rifles, firing carelessly, inaccurately, with a fire that was only deadly because of its intensity; some of the bullets went clipping through the leaves with sharp pit-pit sounds high above his head, and sometimes they thudded with a duller sound into the giant logs behind which they were sheltering.

Michael, seven years old, kept lifting his head up to see what was going on, and Willis said repeatedly: "*Down, keep down, don't move...*" He pushed his feet at the heavy branches behind him, forcing a shelter out of them, worming a way deep into the ground like a hunted animal, and the enormity of the attack brought a kind of desperation to him. It was no longer the question: Could he hold them off? He knew that this was now impossible, and there was a terrible desperation in the knowledge.

It was not the first time he had faced the Mau Mau. The raids had grown in intensity, and two of the servants had deserted. He had fired all the others, except the faithful Adoula (and even him, he had watched most carefully, sitting at dinner with a revolver in his lap), and had sent the farm workers back to their villages, letting the farm go to ruin rather than have the workers face the terrible question that all the Africans were now facing: *Shall I have to kill my master?*

Twice they had attacked his house, but the barricades were strong and the communications system was good, and help had come in plenty of time, long before much damage had been done. It had almost become a pattern, a pattern so clear-cut that when he had said to Dorothy one night: "I think you'd better take Michael to England, darling," she had answered brusquely: "And leave all this behind us?"

"No, not me. Just you and the boy."

She bent forward and kissed him, and said: "We cleared this land together, and we'll hold it together..."

And it had not been hard, either. There had been some terrible atrocities quite close by, but the Willis farm... His beacons were good, the sandbags firm, and the barbed wire which they had strung out

119

together had kept the firebrands at a distance; and he was the best shot in the country and they knew it.

But in the forest... It was broad daylight, and with the carelessness of too much assurance they had strayed from the house, all three of them, three or four miles into the woods where Michael knew there was a family of tiny dik-dik that had lost their mother; he had taken along his rifle merely as a matter of habit, with no more than a dozen rounds in his pocket, and the sudden ambush, the thoughtless stupidity of his unpreparedness had come as a startling shock... Alone, he would have fought and run, run and fought, but with a seven-year-old child...

And now, the last hope was irretrievably gone. He kept saying to himself over and over: *With one bullet, can I kill them both with one bullet?* For it was no longer a question of survival, it was a question, rather, of painlessness.

The hope was gone, gone in the first few minutes when the violent and unexpected surprise of the ambush hit him like a solid blow to the heart; and now the only thing that remained was to negate the pain, the cruelty, the horror...

His wife was staring at him, her face white, and he said quietly: "Dorothy?"

She looked away, and he knew that she had understood the despair on his face. She said: "Don't let Michael know."

"Of course not. There's nothing else, you know that."

She nodded and began to speak, but then they came at him again, eight or nine of them, yelling and waving their *pangas*, and he killed three quickly with fast, accurate shots before they fell back again, and for a tiny moment there was silence, with only the soft noise of the dripping water on the air. And then they began to creep forward again, silently, carefully, full of terrible menace. She said urgently: "Now, do it now, while the resolve is on you."

He counted his ammunition again, knowing there were eight rounds left and trying, by repeated counting, to make it nine, or ten, or a hundred. How long could eight rounds last?

He looked at his watch and at the filtering sun that was still reflected hotly from the gray rock beside them, striking back at the gap in the foliage which had let the bright rays through, steaming the moisture on the ground where it struck and passed on, and he knew that there were still many long hours before they could creep away in darkness...to what?

With a seven-year-old boy who had not yet learned to move through the bush like an animal? With a boy to whom like was a noisy, bright, and cheerful thing, not a shadowed horror to hide from?... And the Mau Mau...could the three of them, hope to move among those preying animals in silence, and escape through three deep miles of heavy forest to...to what?

Beyond was the open country of the farm, and open country was more deadly than the bush. The men of the Mau Mau, the hidden people, could hear a gazelle breathing; they could see an ant move in the darkness; and they could follow a spoor so well that they could tell, by looking at a footprint on the rocks, whether the woman who had made it had been carrying a load of firewood on her head or was merely pregnant.

There was nothing that could save them now. Nothing. There was a finality in the word that he had never really understood before.

The immense love for the silent hurt in her eyes welled up inside him.

She said steadily: "If it begins again, there may not be time..."

He could not bear to look at them. "I've still got a few rounds."

"Eight."

So she had been counting, too. If he had not known before, he knew now. He looked at Michael, strangely silent and fearless, as though he were too young, not too young to know the viciousness of what was happening, but too young to know the sadness of death. *Accepting it,* he thought, *accepting it like an animal.*

The lion will make its kill on the edge of the zebra herd, and after a few moments of panic the others will not move away; they will stand and watch with complete unconcern while the great yellow teeth tear at the still-living, still-kicking flesh, listening to the screams but paying no further heed; their time will surely come, too.

The boy's eyes were composed and untroubled, as though the great expectancy of life were still there, long ahead of him; as if, perhaps, it no longer mattered. The tousled hair hung down over his neck and needed a barber, and there was a scratch on his arm where one of the tame cheetah cubs had scratched him; the hair on his legs was the fair down of extreme youth.

Willis looked again at Dorothy and nodded, letting her know that neither of them would suffer, that the bodies on which the sharp *pangos* would inflict their atrocities would be dead bodies, shot neatly, cleanly, honorably, a quick and painless death and a sudden end to all the nameless filth that was out there.

He said aloud, quite softly, his voice heavy with pain: "You will not suffer, either of you, I promise you that you will not suffer."

And then, unexpectedly, quite unconcerned, the boy, at seven years old, said: "You'll have to kill us, Father, won't you?" As if reading his thoughts he said: "I remember what Mr. Bagley said, after they killed his wife..."

The calm of it cut into his heart like a knife, and he could not reply. But the boy looked at him for an answer, and he forced himself to smile and say: "We keep fighting, Michael. That's a thing you never stop doing. When you have to, you keep on fighting." He forced himself to smile, as though he had no cares in the world, and with their death in his heart he said: "I love you both too much to let them get near you."

And then, they came again. It was the third attack, and the last.

One of the Mau Mau had climbed high into a baobab tree that was close beside them. Its trunk was huge, a full twelve feet across, and they had driven short lengths of thorn twigs into the soft, pulpy mass of it, around on the other side where he could neither see nor hear them, forcing the pegs slowly, by hand, into the pith-like body of the tree, and then one of them had stealthily clambered up till he reached the overhang of the high limbs, moving silently, darkly, like an ape, until his loincloth caught in a twig and tore, and at the sound...

Willis heard the rip of the bark cloth and threw himself sideways, firing up at the same instant, but then it was too late. The black body crashed to the ground, and the grenade that was clenched in its hand went off, and, at the same precise moment of time, some spears came over the barricade, and a piece of metal seared into his leg, almost painlessly.

He swung around to fire at a group of six or seven Kikuyus who were leaping over the fallen logs and racing towards them, and he saw that Dorothy had been hit by a spear that had pinned her hand to the ground; she was staring at the blood in shock, and the boy began to scream in terror.

He fired again and again and again, and Dorothy pulled at the spear, holding it by the blade; in a moment of crazy coherence he wondered why she didn't get hold of the wooden shaft instead, and then he fired twice more and knew that only one round was left and that he could no longer shoot at them. And still, they were coming, less than fifteen yards away.

He swung his rifle and clubbed at one of them who leaped into the shelter, and he felt the skull shatter under the blow, and the pain in his leg hit him and tore him to the ground, and he reeled over and shrieked: "Hold him, hold Michael, tight!"

And there was silence again, and he could not tell if they were still coming, because there was blood in his eyes, and the sound was broken only by the boy's whimpering.

All sense of time had gone with the pain, and it was a sound that caused the silence, but he could not tell if he had heard it or if it had been an imagining out of the past, out of his own incoherence. It was a piercing blast of a trumpet, a jazz trumpet, a Judgment Day trumpet, or perhaps the mad beat of the Jamaican with the wide grin in the London club where they had celebrated their engagement; the sound of the trumpet came to him again, and with it the momentary vision of the impudent, sweaty trumpeter's face, and now the face was close beside him and the light had gone from it with the grenade blast that had torn the chest open, to display the ribs, and the blast of the sound was splitting his ears and he knew that there was only a moment of semi consciousness left, and he yelled again: "Hold on to your mother, Michael, hold on to her tight..."

He tried not to look at the horror on the boy's face as he clutched at his mother, and he thrust the barrel of the rifle close into his back and screamed once: "Dorothy!" and pulled the trigger and saw that the shot had shattered both their hearts before he fell back and lost consciousness, the sound of the trumpeter still ringing back and forth in the blackness of coma.

But the sound was real.

There were three short blasts on a bugle, less than half a mile away, and then four more that meant: *Move to the west.*

A platoon and a half of the Queen's African Rifles, their shiny leather dulled, their helmets covered with coarse grass, came charging towards the sound of the shots and the exploding grenade, and the attack was over, over as quickly as it had begun, with nothing left but tortured bodies, black and white, on the green forest floor, and the sure knowledge that the humus would swallow up the terror until it was ready to erupt again.

When Willis came to his senses, his lower stomach had been tightly bound with broad white bandages, and there was a padded splint on his left leg.

For a while, staring at the ceiling, afraid to ask for the truth, he tried to sort out in his own mind the shadings of fact and fantasy, understanding at last the terrible thing that he had done and fighting the conscious memory of it.

He fought, too, against the medicines, but the doctors were too strong for him, and his own body, in turn, fought the twisted deliberations of his own will.

Three months later, still on crutches, he went back to the big house that he and Dorothy had built, almost unaided, on the clearing they had torn from the encroaching bush in the early, struggling days, and he set fire to it.

He turned loose the two-year-old lion the boy had once played with, and while the sole remaining servant, Adoula, stared in silent blankness, he had carried burning brands into the house and thrown them about, and fired the pyrethrum fields and the barns, and had set a charge of dynamite under the tall water tower that had taken him two years to build.

And then he had sat on an outcrop of rock and watched the destruction of his life's work, watching the flames and the smoke that slowly darkened the sky, and he had cried, silently, alone, and in terrible pain.

PART THREE

The Gateway to Sorrow

CHAPTER 9

After the night, the desert was awakening, and the early sun was gold on the walls of Darhuzuni.

Their rifles ready, Marion, Willis, and Babajee moved out of the house and into the sunlight. For a while they stood looking down into the depths of the old well.

Babajee said eagerly: "There's no one else could get down there, Mr. Willis, only a thin man like me, isn't it?"

Willis nodded, looking at Babajee with affection. "It won't be very easy down there, you know that? And there'll always be the danger of a cave-in."

"But we *must* get water. There is no other way."

"There'll be two of us out here all the time you're down there, covering you. And if we start shooting, Tabor and M'Butu and Bradley will all start firing from the roof as well, so there's nothing to worry about. Just keep digging, and up here we'll keep our fingers crossed. I'll haul up the sand in the bucket, but I'll have my rifle close by, and Marion...hell, she's a better shot than I am."

"Oh, I am not worried at all," Babajee said. "It is just that...my daughter is a little frightened for me."

"She knows she can trust me too."

"Yes, yes, I know that."

Was there a breath of suspicion there? Willis sighed and thought: *You can never tell what they are really thinking.*

Babajee pushed his arms through the loop in the rope, and stepped gingerly over the side. He had thrown down the collapsible shovel from the truck, hearing the soft thud as it landed in dry sand.

There was a moment of fright as he put his weight on the rope, scratching at the concrete sides with his feet, and then Willis gently began to lower him, playing the line out slowly.

Marion took her eyes off Willis to watch the desert, and she said quietly: "Somewhere out there, they're watching us."

Almost automatically, she looked back at the house to see if the others were there. M'Butu, high on the roof, looked down at her and waved, and she could see Tabor and Bradley carefully posted at the two extremes of the gables, watching.

She said to Willis: "Where's Carrierco? He should be doing that."

Willis turned and grimaced at her. He said: "Mr. Carrierco is keeping out of sight. He's not too anxious to show himself."

"He must know they're pretty lousy shots, and a long way off at that. They're his own people."

"Exactly, his own people."

The slight wind was blowing her hair across her face as she stood there with her feet apart, her gun cradled in her arms, a slim blonde Diana. She frowned and said: "They know he's here. What the hell's he trying to do?"

"Just not to let the *watu* see him working for us too hard."

As if he had heard the comment, Carrierco came out of the house, omitting to say that Tabor had sent him, and said affably: "Let me do that, Mr. Willis, let me take the rope. I feel that they just might come at us if they see us working. And if they do..."

"All right. Keep pulling up the buckets as fast as Babajee can fill them. We'll get over by the wall, just in case."

Willis handed him the rope and took Marion's slender arm. He said: "Over here, we're under cover and there's a good field of view."

She pulled away from him and while he waited, secretly amused, she went to the well, leaned over its brim, and called down into the darkness: "Mr. Babajee? Willis and I are covering you from the wall. Carrierco's on the rope, all right?"

The answer was muted, indistinct, hesitant. Babajee looked up at the round patch of skylight, terrifyingly high above him, and called out: "It is very hot down here. Very dry, too." His voice was hollow.

126

"I know. You want some water? Shall I send you down half a bottle?"

"No, thank you, really, it is not necessary."

"All right. Good luck."

In the depths of the confining shaft, Babajee sighed, and began to strip off his clothes. He folded them neatly, found a broken piece of stonework to serve as a shelf, placed them carefully, and dug his shovel into the soil.

Each time the heavy bucket went slowly up, he sat back on his haunches, sweating, panting, and acutely miserable.

He said aloud: "Really, if my friends could see me now, working like a savage..."

He thought of the bright, colorful house in town, of the comfortable Asian Social Club where the pink lemonade was always ice-cold, served by men like Carrierco in neat white costumes; and he thought of the big sisal estate with its huge verandas and honeysuckled patio... The workers had   rioted there a few weeks ago, and the thought of their sudden savagery brought tears to his eyes. He forced himself to think of his home, and he went on digging.

All day long Babajee toiled at the digging in his dark pit, and the sand remained obstinately dry.

Carrierco, torn between his desire not to be seen working and his knowledge of the distrust that Tabor and the others had for him, muttered to himself as he hauled on the rope at the top, emptying the sand in an ever-growing heap beside the well. From time to time he stared out into the desert, looking at the silent gray scrub, knowing the *watu* were still there, patiently waiting...for what? He wondered how circumstance had forced him to throw in his lot with the old M'Butu and the older Willis. *Old men*, he said contemptuously, *old men who will soon be as dead as the shadow of the past they live in...* He stopped working once when he felt the sweat would no longer come out of his body, and went into the house. He said to Willis hopelessly: "One small mug of water, Mr. Willis, please..."

Tabor was lashing two heavy rafters together with a length of rope. He said sourly: "You know what the ration is, Carrierco."

"Yes, Mr. Tabor, but physical work like that..."

"If Babajee can manage without, so can you. You'll have to. You get another mouthful this evening."

Willis got up and took one of the water bottles and handed it to him, and said, not looking at Tabor: "A mouthful and that's all. A small one at that."

Carrierco drank carefully, and when he had gone out into the hot bright sunshine again, Willis said calmly: "All right, one or two of us haven't been drinking any at all. You too. We've got a little in hand."

Tabor only grunted, and went on with tying his knots. He said at last: "How far down are they?"

"About three feet. It's slow work."

"Still dry?"

"Still dry."

"I'm beginning to worry about it."

"And so am I."

And so was Carrierco. As he waited for the sixty-fourth bucket to be filled, he stared out into the desert, wondering. He looked up at the gables and saw Marion standing guard, with the Indian girl who had just relieved Bradley holding her incongruous rifle as though she were frightened of it.

He looked to the desert again, and knew they were out there watching him, and the temptation was strong to leave the rope, to throw up his hands and run towards them, to say to them: "I am your friend, I am the man who helped you..."

But he knew that he dared not. Not in daylight, at least. He went on wearily hauling at the rope. The buckets of sand that came up were still dry.

When the sun went down on the day and the night set in, a creeping despondency came slowly over them for the first time. Babajee came out of the well, exhausted, frustrated, and close to tears. But be said stubbornly: "I will go down again in the morning. I will go down and keep digging until we find it. Somewhere under the sand there must be water, I know it. And I will find it for you."

128

Willis began to worry that the solution to their problem was not as simple as it had seemed at first. Staring out into the darkness, he said: "Another night? I would not have believed it."

He was aware of a kind of impatient reproachfulness in Tabor's manner, as though the American had known, all along, that they were deeper in trouble than some of them had imagined; as though, from the viewpoint of his distant detachment, he could more clearly see the forces that were gathering against them.

But if Tabor could, they did not seem to perturb him; there was a stubborn acceptance there, an acceptance of an intolerable position that was only going to last until he found the answer—and then no longer.

It seemed to Willis as if the unspoken words were: "I told you, we've got to do something about it, not wait for the luck of the British to come and get us out of this mess."

Tabor said now, looking at Willis as though expecting a rebuff: "I'm going out there to take a look. I want to prowl around for a while."

Willis frowned up at the moon, low on the horizon.

"I wouldn't recommend it... Ten more minutes it'll be as black as pitch out there."

"That's how I like it."

Willis did not want to bring to a head the question that had been plaguing him ever since the time it had first become apparent that, during the first day, they had no hope of getting quickly to safety; sooner or later, he knew, *someone* was going to have to take a more rigid command, to install some military discipline, to bind the forces together and ensure their fullest use; he knew how Tabor would take a flat objection, and he did not want so early to face a division of their diverse authorities.

He said hesitantly: "If you think you can achieve anything..."

Tabor was carefully putting a round into the barrel of his .306 and replacing it with another the chamber. He said (also not wanting to argue): "I might get a chance to see what they look like, what sort of arms they've got. I believe they're waiting for reinforcements, and if that's true, we'd be wise to bust out of here as soon as we can."

And when Willis said: "They're waiting for the witch doctor," Tabor snorted and said nothing. Willis insisted: "It's true, that's what they're waiting for."

"Then maybe I'd better bewitch the bastards myself. Give me a couple of hours, and I'll be back." The gun was ready, the hunting knife sharp as he tested the edge on his thumbnail.

The candle flared in the darkness, and Bradley was there, a match in his hand, his white face glowing with the yellow light. He said unexpectedly: "Don't overrate your talents, Tabor. If you think you can move about among them without being heard, or seen..."

Tabor said: "That's exactly what I think."

Willis made a last effort: "They might just try to force their way in as soon as the moon is down. If they do, we're going to need your rifle."

"If they do that, and maybe they will..." he grinned quickly "...won't they be surprised to hear shooting behind them? They'll turn and run for cover the moment I start to fire."

"All right. How much ammo have you got?"

"I'm taking thirty rounds."

"I still don't like it very much... If anything happens to you..."

Tabor was still grinning at him. "Nothing will. Hell, I can move quietly. You ought to know that, you're the man who taught me."

"I should have taught you common sense as well."

"It's common sense to find out the enemy's strength if you can."

"And I hope you can."

"If I come running and yelling, open the door fast, switch on the light, and keep shooting."

They had taken the headlamps and the battery from the Land Rover, fastening them above the doorway, with the switch inside by the window, to make a sort of searchlight.

Willis said desperately: "But for God's sake, be careful! They can see in the dark like cats..."

"Baloney. If there's a single word for this goddam country it's inefficiency. There's nothing they can do that I can't do better, and that includes crawling around the goddam bush in the night. That's something else I learned."

130

When the moon was down and the blackness was complete, he slipped through the door, over the low wall, and disappeared.

They watched the darkness close about him like a black fog, and Willis said irritably: "Get on the switch, Bradley. First unholy sound, I want all the light we can get."

Tabor would never have believed that the darkness could be so intense, nor the silence so acute. It was something he had never understood about the bush at night; that at one moment the sounds of the animals, and the insects, and the birds could be so loud as to almost deafen him, bursting in a crescendo that sometimes seemed to split his eardrums; and then, in the next sudden moment, a silence could descend so absolute that with it came all the old ancestral fears from the depths of his primeval instincts.

The fear in the silence seemed to abnegate his thousand years of culture, and make him again one with the animals, and one with the savage black men he was stalking, as though the great gulf between them had been wrenched away by a savage, hostile environment.

He sat still on the cold sand for a while, looking up at the stars and knowing that the danger came not only from the *watu* but also from his own assurance. He said to himself moodily: "That jerk Bradley..."

He placed the North Star carefully, and Orion's belt, and the Milky Way, and knew that if, after his excursion, he moved due southeast towards the sea, he would hit the cliffs somewhere, and then Darhuzuni would be...north a few hundred yards? Or south?

He said to himself: "Due northwest for five hundred paces, no more, then circle round, not too far and not too long... Then, due southeast to the sea again." It was so dark that the luminous dial of his watch gleamed greenly on his wrist, and he turned it around to hide it.

He got to his feet and began to walk, with infinite patience, into the darkness, moving one pace at a time and feeling the ground before trusting his weight on it, just as Willis had taught him to do the night they went out after the big leopard, testing his weight and the ground too, feeling for twigs or stones that might, if he were careless, break the meticulous silence. He had taken off his shoes and was walking barefoot, knowing the difference, as the animals knew, between *quiet* and *absolute* silence, between the quiet in which a man's breathing can be heard at a hundred paces, and the absolute silence in which there is nothing but a complete and utter loneliness.

His bare foot turned a tiny pebble and he heard it; a good hunter, he froze. Another sound came to him—a slight, sharp sound that was someone moving in Darhuzuni, the other side of the wall, the other side of the house, three hundred yards away towards the sea.

He could not hear the waves below the cliff, and he knew that the water was a sheet of glass again. He heard Petna's voice, low, soft, controlled, but clear on the breeze: "I am afraid for him."

The answer was a zephyr, quite indistinguishable. Was it Willis she was speaking to? Only Willis among them had learned to speak without projection, so that his whisper could not be heard more than twenty feet away.

Then the breeze shifted and carried the murmuring away from him and out to sea.

The dark sky was an immensity above him, the sand an immensity around him, spreading out from the focal point of his feet into an infinity that was unbroken save by patches of struggling dry scrub that were even now sucking at the transient dampness of the night air, an immense infinity that was silent, deserted, empty, and frightening. And only darkness covered it all, a darkness in which the stars seemed closer than the earth, because the stars could be seen and the ground at his feet could not.

He moved slowly, pace after silent pace, counting his steps, listening, waiting, watching. And soon, in the incalculable distance, he saw their fire.

It came to his sight suddenly, unexpectedly, and when he moved back a step, it had gone; he knew then that it was hidden among the rocks that shielded it from the house. He could not even smell the smoke, and it seemed as if this, too, were part of the conspiracy of loneliness.

He moved forward again, finding the flames, then over to one side, till he was sure he could keep it just out of his sight but within his knowledge, and he began to move towards it, straining his ears and his eyes and his sense of smell. A hundred yards, seventy-five, fifty... Somewhere here there would be a sentry, must *surely* be a sentry.

Moving slowly, more slowly than ever before, he walked into an unseen outcrop of jagged limestone, and cursed soundlessly at the infinitesimal breaking of the silence. Here, he knew, was where the sentry could be, up there above him, listening in the motionless air.

He dug his bare toes into the sand and he waited. The grit was cold under his feet, finding its way between his toes, and now the gentle sound of the surf came to him again on the shifting breeze, and with it came a nebulous memory out of the past, an image that could not reach the clarity of his thought but remained a disturbing image... A touch, a scent, a sound? Something was at the edge of his mind, nudging his brain for recognition, and he brushed it aside, almost angrily, forcing himself to concentrate on the flame-lit black bodies that were so dangerously close to him.

Some of them were standing limply around, relaxed, leaning against the rocks in silence. Some were in rags, and some wore crumpled khaki uniforms, ill-fitting as though they had been looted from some military store, and one or two wore the old-fashioned tribal regalia, though he could not identify their tribes.

Some of them were smoking cigarettes, crouching on their heels in the silence, muttering an occasional guttural sound that he could not understand, staring into the flames and waiting.

Peering around the bluff, keeping his weight steadily on the balls of both feet, he counted them; eight, ten, twelve; six (or was it seven?) out there by the trees, scarcely illuminated as more than shadows; eighteen or nineteen in the immediate circle of fire... And further out there...how many?

Most of them were quite young, no more than twenty years old, their bodies shining redly in the flames. Some of them had rifles (he counted them: nine), and some of them had *pangas* at their sides; some of them held their spears loosely in their dejected hands, sticking up like emblems between their up-thrust knees; one of them was honing a knife on a piece of granite, the gentle scraping sound of it coming softly to him. They all had tribal markings on their brown, shining faces.

One of them, a heavily built man in an Army officer's cap, was

133

examining some hand grenades, British Mills bombs, which he was taking from his pockets and carefully unwrapping.

Tabor thought gruffly: *If we only had a few of those, just one is all we need to sort this lot out...* Watching in the darkness, he wondered for a while if a sudden charge and a grab at the grenades would be fruitful, but he knew that he would never get away far enough to use them, and he thrust the idea away from him, regretfully but firmly.

He moved softly away, towards the other side of the bluff. There was another group of them here, a little apart from the others, and they carried spears and short, inefficient bows with leather quivers full of tiny poisoned arrows; there was not a rifle among them. He frowned and counted them carefully: eleven.

And then, as he watched, there were two quick shots from Darhuzuni, and they were suddenly springing to their feet, looking, not at him but out there in the darkness towards the house. In a moment, they were gone from the fires, moving so swiftly and so silently that it seemed their presence there a moment ago had been a mirage. He drew back quickly, worrying about what the shooting was for.

And then, in the absolute silence, he was conscious of an alien scent. He drew back close to the bluff, taking his eyes quickly off the fire and closing them to wipe out the momentary blindness; there was no sound, and when he opened his eyes again there was nothing to see, nothing but an impenetrable darkness in which even the stars seemed remote, detached, and unfriendly.

Silence. Nothing. Limbo.

Only the scent was still there, the strong scent of a man hiding close by in the obscurity, a scent that seemed to taunt him, to mock him with its constancy. He moved away slowly, with infinite patience, in a quiet that was absolute, in a darkness that was complete.

And then, suddenly, the stench came on him with a rush and there was a flurry of movement around him; in a primeval instinct he threw up his left arm to guard his head, and he felt the sharp sting of a *panga* cutting into his forearm; he could smell his own blood, and he lashed out hard with his fist, a fist that still gripped the stock of his rifle, and he felt the hard, polished walnut crash into flesh and a body went down, and someone yelled out there by the fire, and he knew that there was only a moment or two left...

He dropped quickly to the ground, feeling for the body that was beside him, feeling the warm life still tingling in it, listening to the harsh, staccato breathing and knowing that it was a beacon to guide the others. His finger's gripped a handful of wet, grease-stinking hair and twisted the motionless head around, and then he dropped his rifle beside him and put his hands around the throat and silently began to choke away the life that was there.

The flesh was soft under his hands, and he could feel the ridges on the windpipe, and he crushed his hands together so strongly that the fingers and thumbs were almost meeting, separated only by a resilient layer of flesh that was motionless, passive, unresisting under his powerful grasp. He could see the fallen *panga* close beside him, reflecting the firelight; the blood on it was his own blood, and the slash on his arm, so deep that the bone was exposed, began to pain him furiously...

And then the helpless hands began to clutch at his, and the legs thrashed out, and the body struggled, and there was suddenly a terrible alarm on him, a hateful despondency, and the nebulous memory took sudden form with the startling clarity of an accusation, an accusation that was directed against the murderous strength in his hands. He said to himself angrily, shocked into bewildered protest: "But he tried to kill me, for God's sake..."

But the hesitation was enough. Because he could not, in his own mind, clearly separate the reason from the passion, he thrust the still-living body away from him, and ran, crouching low, fast, into the darkness towards the three stars that hung in the black sky like jewels below Orion's belt, running fast across the thirsty sand until he came to the walls of Darhuzuni.

Afterwards, he could not imagine what subtle force it was that had made him hesitate. He found the *panga* in his hand and did not know that he had even stopped to pick it up, and he slung his rifle over his shoulder and fingered the razor edge of the blade. He heard them running now, the soft padding of their feet out there somewhere, and he went quickly, not bothering to move silently anymore, up to the gate of the house.

When he whistled once, Willis opened the door and let him in, and he threw the *panga* down with a clatter on the floor and said moodily: "A trophy. It's not much, is it?"

Marion said: "My God, your arm..." And he grimaced and held it up to stop the blood coming, and while he sat down in the light of the candle, she sprinkled the wound with sulfanilamide and bound it tight with a bandage.

Then the lights outside went on as Petna pulled the switch and called out: "I think they're coming..."

Tabor and Willis reached for their guns, but by the time they found their posts by the windows there was nothing out there but darkness again.

Willis said sharply: "Put out the light at once if anyone fires."

Tabor looked at him and raised his eyebrows, and Willis said: "You'll see."

He held a broken pane of glass in his hand, and Tabor nodded and said: "Oh."

They stared out to the edges of the circle of yellow light; nothing moved. Willis said: "Is the arm all right?"

Tabor grunted, not taking his eyes away from the bushes. "Worse things have happened."

"Down to the bone, it looked pretty bad."

Tabor flexed his fingers. "I'll live."

There was quiet for a while. Willis said at last: "Just to cheer you up... Carrierco's gone."

"Gone!" Tabor stared at him in disbelief. "He doesn't really think he can get away, does he? They're all around us out there."

"Some of them are his friends."

Again, the long silence.

Tabor said: "Any damage before he went?"

"No. I had the water bottles with me. He took his Luger, of course."

"Mr. goddam Carrierco. He shows his head just once, I'll blow it off his goddam shoulders."

"M'Butu saw him run out of the house and fired a couple of shots after him, but it was too dark..."

"So that's what it was. Well, we're better off without him, the hell with him." Tabor thought for a moment and said softly: "He knows we can't hold out for long without water."

"They know that already. They've seen us digging out the well."

"But he also knows we've got plenty of ammunition."

Willis said slowly: "M'Butu told me, 'When Carrierco leaves us, we'll know the odds have become too strong.' I wonder if he was right?" Tabor merely snorted.

Willis fingered his sheet of glass and muttered: "Come on, come on, what are you waiting for?"

In a moment, the firing began, erratic, unsteady, harmless, but still they could see nothing but the flashes of the rifles. It went on for a little while and Willis called out: "Ready, Petna!... Now!"

At the precise moment that Petna switched off the headlamps, Willis dropped the pane of glass to the concrete floor and let it shatter noisily, and then he said softly: "Wait till I shout for it..."

Marion crept in beside them and whispered anxiously: "Was that the lamp? Did they hit it?"

Willis shook his head and said: "Watch now, a lesson in strategy."

Tabor was counting the seconds: "Three...four...five...six... seven..."

And Willis said: "Ready? Now, Petna!"

Petna threw the switch again and the picture out there was startlingly different, a picture of arrested motion... Eight or nine of them, caught moving swiftly towards the house, were bent double, startled into immobility, their weapons unready, staring in surprise at the light. One of them, moving faster than the others, yelled out and broke into a run for the house, firing a magazine shotgun as he came and pumping the chamber empty, and then the rest of the picture exploded into spotlit action. The guns began firing, and a spear came thudding into the timber of the door to bury itself deeply, forced deep by the weight of the solid iron shaft.

For a moment, Willis felt a touch of admiration for them as they charged, moving like scuttling rabbits towards them, eight, nine, ten, twelve of them, yelling and charging and waving their weapons. Another group of eight or nine was out in the flank, further away. One of them dropped quickly to his knee and loosed three tiny arrows in rapid succession, but they fell short; a fourth lodged into a mullion of the window, the poison dripping from its point in a brown, sickly trickle.

Tabor said clearly: "All right, let's take them before they get any closer."

He fired quickly, expertly, hearing the echo of his shots as Willis and Marion fired beside him.

The attack broke up as the *watu* changed their minds and ran back for cover, and one of them dropped behind the protective wall of the well, and four of them lay dead on the sand...

Willis said: "There's one by the wall, can you see him?"

Tabor shook his head. "I saw him drop there, but he's out of sight."

Willis said calmly: "So hold your fire, he won't stay there long."

"He'll stay till the battery runs down and the lamps go out."

"No. He knows we'll be out there soon, outflanking him. I'll take him when he moves out."

Almost as soon as he spoke, the shadow moved, and there was a sudden dash across the desert; he ran, a small, wiry African with a spear and a rifle in his hands, running fast across the bush, faster than any man can run who is not driven by his own desperation, so fast that when Willis' single shot sounded, the body rolled over and over, carried on by its own momentum till it lay still in the cloud of dust that gathered about it and hung there in the glare of the lamp.

Watching, Bradley whispered: "Five of them in less than a minute. Won't they *learn?*..."

Willis was worried, puzzled about the determination they had shown. He said slowly: "They're stronger than we thought. I'd have sworn they wouldn't dare. And once they've started...will they stop?"

"They were sitting by the fire there," Tabor said, "with all the time in the world. Waiting. For what? For reinforcements?"

Willis did not answer him.

In Mwadi, thirty miles away, the reinforcements were getting ready.

The fragile old man came slowly out of his hut, supported by three of his bodyguards. One of them was Owadi, the son of Bakulu, a good warrior and a practical, placid, assured man with heavy shoulders and hard biceps. Those who knew him (among them, Peter Tarutu and John Carrierco) saw in him a degree of sophistication that belied his close association with the witch doctor, and it was assumed that he worked with the old man only for the power it gave him.

The three slowly dressed the old man in his ceremonial robes. A leopard skin was put over his shoulders, and tied with a waistband of zebra skin which was intended to show that his men, at least, had learned the closely guarded Masai secret (never learned even by the white man) of tanning the zebra hide and making it soft as silk. There were ostrich feathers bound around his head with a band of plaited gut, and elephant hair was bound around his biceps; stripes of white paint had been carefully laid across his thin, rib-shadowed chest. Around his throat there was a long string of lion's claws, and a rope of small white ceramic pebbles, once painted in bright colors, that had been brought to these shores by Portuguese traders more than five centuries ago, and for which, many long years past, he had bartered one of the tribal virgins with the Somalis across the border. What was left of his hair (for he was very old) had been plastered at the back of his neck with a mixture of wood-ash and urine, and he carried a small club which was bound at the handle with the intestines of a cat.

As the warriors dressed him, the other villagers sat by the doors and waited, fearfully, for the ceremonial robes could only mean trouble for someone; and trouble for *someone* usually found its way back to the tribe.

He was a man who held the power of life and death in his skinny, angry hand, a man the simple tribesmen went out of their way to avoid, a man whose wicked glance was enough to fill them all with abject terror.

He was a man without whose help no evil course could ever be run, whose magic roused the warriors to a pitch of fanatical jury, whose *uchawi* protected them in battle, and whose incantations gave them the powers of the devils.

He was a sick, angry, evil old man. He was the Witch Doctor.

CHAPTER 10

Carrierco could not help chuckling to himself in the darkness. He walked through the night with no attempt at silence, looking back once or twice at the old house and thinking of that ape M'Butu. He had said to him, at the end of the long day's work: "They won't give me any more water, M'Butu, and it's been a long day out there in the sun."

M'Butu had eyed him evenly. "You were digging for water. So why do you ask me to give you some?"

"Because we didn't find it, of course. The well's dry, dry as a bone."

M'Butu said: "I gave my ration to the Indian girl. Her fear has dried her body like a goatskin."

Carrierco looked at him in astonishment. "To the Indian girl? Now I know you are too old. Give me some water, grandfather."

"No."

"Old man, your granddaughter is my wife! I am your kin! Give me some water!"

M'Butu looked at him and grinned, and as Carrierco stared the grin widened until the old man was shaking with his pleasure. He said, laughing: "The old days, Carrierco, in the old days we learned how to suffer! But now we are all children, children who do not know how to resist. You learned to drive a truck, you learned to argue and make speeches, and you have forgotten the hardness that is our heritage. Even the white men you despise so much are not complaining about their thirst, and you know why? Because they are

Africans."

Carrierco said scornfully: "The American too?"

"Even the American. Even the Memsahib. They can resist because they know that here, inside a man, is all the force that his gods have given him, the force to fight and the force to resist... You are a weakling, Carrierco, a child screaming for a worthless toy."

"I saved your life, old man. If I had not come to Mwadi..."

M'Butu sighed. "Yes, and I have looked hard for the reason. The white men do not know it, but...there are many of your friends out there, do you deny it?"

"No, I do not." Carrierco fell silent for a while. He said at last, sullenly: "Once, some of them were my friends. But they no longer listen to reason..."

"Your kind of reason."

"My kind of reason. So now I am one of you. So give me your waterskin."

M'Butu shook his grizzled head. He said gently: "We are all thirsty. We will be more thirsty before this trouble is over."

Carrierco had trembled, but controlled his anger. Fingering the Luger that was stuck in his belt under the heavy overcoat, he knew now that the time had come for him to leave.

And now, still chuckling in the silence of the bush, he pulled up short when the shadows he had seen stirring ahead of him resolved themselves into four short, thickset men.

The Luger in his hand was steady, and they looked at it and waited, and he said clearly: "I want to see the man who is in command here."

One of them grunted something at him in a dialect he did not understand, and he stifled the impatience and said, knowing they did not speak Swahili, but only their tribal dialect: "*Jumbe*, the man who is your chief." When one of them raised a threatening *panga*, he said again loudly: "*Jumbe*, the chief, *Jumbe!*"

Behind him, he had heard nothing. But then, a heavy hand took hold of his shoulder and spun him around, and an African who was not from this part of the country, not, perhaps, from this country at all, glared at him and said in Swahili: "I am the chief, the Captain. Why do you bring yourself to me? A sacrifice?" His Swahili was thick, strange, accented.

Carrierco gestured at the gun in his hand and said: "I bring you another weapon with which to fight the white men." But he did not hand it over.

It was cocked, and ready to fire, and the Captain looked at it scornfully and said: "You are the man Carrierco. You sold us two hundred rifles, and now you give me a toy pistol."

"I have come to help you, to tell you that the white men have no water. In a day or two... All you have to do is wait."

The Captain said: "Everyone tells me what to do. Why did you take M'Butu from Mwadi?"

Carrierco hesitated, but his story was ready. He said, shrugging: "You know how it is..."

"I do not know."

"He is my grandfather. If I did not make a token effort to help him, my wife would never sleep with me again."

"I will sleep with her instead, when you are dead."

Carrierco, gauging this man's worth, was not afraid of him. He said: "You will gain nothing by killing me, you know that. Better to let me fight with you against them."

"Will you charge into their guns, as my men have been charging?"

"Of course not!" Carrierco said scornfully. "I am not a fool. It is better to keep your distance, and to pick them off one by one as they show their heads above the wall. All day, for two days, they have been out in the open, and not one of your warriors has yet killed a single one of them."

"And you can do this?"

"Yes."

"At three hundred yards? You are a fool, Carrierco."

"Even at three hundred yards, with a little care..."

The Captain took another tack: "Where did you get your pistol?"

Carrierco shrugged. "A long time ago. You must remember that I sometimes carried your men from the forest when the police were looking for them."

"Not you. Your men."

"Because I told them to."

"And the pistol?"

"For my own protection, no more."

"Against whom?"

"Against the police, of course."

A note of unease was creeping into Carrierco's voice. He said, speaking quickly and easily: "In a fight like this, you need all the help you can get, and I happen to be in a privileged position. I know the enemy, and I know their weaknesses. With me to help you..."

"You would not have used the pistol against my men if they had attacked you?"

Carrierco said uncomfortably: "Why should they attack me?"

"Because you work for the white man."

"Not *for* him. I steal from him. With me to help you..."

"Will you give me the pistol now?" The Captain's eyes were sharp, alert, amused.

Carrierco swallowed hard and drove away an encroaching fear: "Yes, if you really want it. But it is better that I keep it if I am to work with you. With me to help you, the struggle against the enemy..."

"Give me the gun."

Carrierco hesitated, saw there was no way out of his predicament, and forced a smile. "Of course." He flipped back the breech, caught the ejected shell expertly, slipped out the magazine, and handed the magazine and the pistol to the Captain.

He said affably: "Take it as a present. It is a good gun, a very good gun."

"We shall see how good it is," the Captain said nonchalantly, but watching him closely. "I have sent for our friend from Mwadi to help us."

"Our friend?" Carrierco looked at him blankly.

"Our friend. When he comes, I am sure he would like to see you. And for my part, I would like to make him a present, too."

While Carrierco stared at him in bewilderment, the Captain gave an order, and one of the men stepped forward and knocked him to the ground with the heavy shaft of his spear. Before he could struggle to his feet again, they had seized his arms, twisted them behind his back and tied them tightly with a loop around his throat, and bound his knees together with strips of hide.

As they began to drag him towards the fire, he felt the blood draining out of his face. He shouted once: "I have helped you, I am the man who gave you trucks, and men, and money...!"

The Captain stepped forward and kicked him in the face, and he fell silent.

The moon was a narrow crescent low in the black sky, and up in the foliage of the acacia tree, crouched like an ape in an angle of the branches, the African who called himself the "Captain" was staring out into the impenetrable darkness. Only his ears and his sense of smell were serving him. To the east there was the faintest grayness in the black of the sky.

He could smell it first, the thick, ripe scent of decaying flesh, and then he could hear the slight shuffle of feet in the sand, far away, no more than a tiny abnegation of the absolute silence; even the night birds had stopped calling each other as if in fear of the approaching litter. He waited till he was sure, and then he dropped quietly to the ground.

He was a squat, strong man of middle age, his ears long-lobed with the ribbon fresh hanging down to his shoulders, and there were three scars down the side of each broad flat cheek. He wore Army shorts, a khaki hunting jacket, and a stolen Army cap on his head, and his pockets were full of hand grenades that he had wrapped in cloth to keep them silent.

He went over to the shadows under the rocks, the darker shadows in the darkness where three of his men lay, and kicked them awake.

He said gruffly: "Get up, our friend is coming." He could sense the quiver of sudden excitement that ran through them, and he said: "Don't be afraid, he is our friend." He could see the fear in the whites of their eyes as they stared at him, and he said irritably: "I sent for him, I told him to come."

They said nothing, watching him fearfully, and his irritation increased. He said: "Get up, we have work to do. And with his help, they will not stop us again."

One of the men, a thin, wasted youth of eighteen, said slowly, fearfully: "It is better we wait till they leave the house, and cut them down in the desert. We have lost eleven of our men. Eleven."

The Captain peered at him, scowling. "You are the son of Obangu?"

"Yes, Obangu is my father."

"Obangu is a brave man. Why is he not with us?"

The youth hesitated. "He is sick, in his bed." It was a lie, but he hoped the Captain would believe him. He said desperately: "His spirit is with us to make us brave."

The Captain turned away and said scornfully: "Our friend will bring us all the spirits we need."

He did not believe in them himself, but he, too, knew the weakness of his frightened men.

The young man began to tie on the shoes which he was slipping over his bare feet, and the Captain looked down at them and said: "You wear shoes in the bush?"

"They gave them to me...at the school."

"A schoolboy. I do not like schoolboys," the Captain growled. "I ask for warriors, and they send me children."

The three men got slowly to their feet, and soon the litter appeared, a heavy chair slung on two poles born by four sweating men. Eight spear-carrying warriors walked beside it, and when the chair was put down, the warriors set aside their spears and went to help the witch doctor to his feet.

They supported him by the fragile arms and set him down on a pile of sand over which one of them threw a blanket, and they waited till his labored breathing came more easily and the slow fire came back to the exhausted eyes; and then they sat down beside him, staring stolidly at the Captain, sure of the privilege of their authority, and knowing that this man was a fool, and a foreign fool at that, for hoping to bring into his service the efforts of the only wise man in the tribe.

At last the witch doctor began to speak. His voice was thin as a reed, high-pitched, stumbling, and he spoke in a rhythmic incantation, as though he were singing a hymn.

He said: "There are seven there...of whom two are women...and one is a coward...and one is an Asian who will do us no harm...and one is a chief who is no longer a chief..." He turned his shriveled head from side to side and said: "How many men have you?"

The Captain was hypnotized by the slow voice, the lethargic movements, the soft incantation. As if suddenly aware of his fascination and shocked by it, he said abruptly: "Thirty-two rifles, many *pangas* and spears."

"How many men?"

The Captain hesitated, angry at his own incompetence. "In all, eighty-seven."

"And twelve have died."

"Eleven."

The old man looked at him, holding up his head with difficulty. His words wheezed through his ancient windpipe: "Twelve."

The Captain did not argue. (He did not know it, but a moment before, one of his men, wounded in the stomach, had quietly died). He said: "You know the old fort. Once it held the British Navy at bay for two weeks. How can I take it with thirty-two rifles in two nights?"

"And so you ask my help."

"Some of my men are frightened. The white men use their guns too well, and we do not know how much ammunition they have."

"And what will you give me for my help?"

The Captain said: "It is not a question of payment. When we have done what we are doing, it will be better for you, too. However..." He looked at the witch doctor's cunning eyes and said: "The man who told M'Butu we were coming for him, Carrierco. He is my prisoner."

The ancient head nodded slowly up and down, and a shudder took hold of the Captain's body; it seemed that the venom there was a poisonous fog that would suffocate him. He knew that he had made a bargain.

For a long, long time there was silence. The old man's eyes were closed, as if he were sleeping, and the Captain waited patiently for him to speak, knowing that if he spoke first the witch doctor would be angry and would not help him.

And then the tiny eyes opened and the small voice came; "They have more than five hundred bullets."

At that precise moment, in the fortress of Darhuzuni, Tabor stood my from his crouched position by the candle, pushed away the last box of ammunition, and said to Willis: "One box of four hundred and eighty rounds, and you and I have thirty each...and a dozen cartridges for the shotguns. Hell, we could hold out forever if we had to."

The witch doctor said softly: "They have no water, and the well is close at hand."

"The well is dry, old man."

"They will try to clean it out. Under so much sand..." (he held out his finger halfway up his forearm) "...there is water."

"Then we will poison it." The Captain jerked his thumb to where, he knew, two of his men were squatting over a tiny fire in the darkness, stewing the roots and the beans of the Strychnos tree, straining the thick red pulp through a crab shell to leave the sticky, deadly residue for the tips of their spears. He said: "I will send one man to creep to the well in the darkness and put poison in it."

"No."

The Captain knew the mistake he had made. He said hastily: "Of course, we will wait until they have dug for the water so that the poison will not be wasted in dry sand."

The witch doctor said: "No. A man must run to the well when they are working there, and he must drop one of your grenades into it, and the men who are inside will be killed."

"They will only work in daylight. In daylight, we cannot approach the well. My men will all be killed."

Again, it seemed that the old man was asleep. The Captain began to speak again, and one of the warriors thrust out a foot and kicked him in the stomach, and he fell silent, glad of the darkness that shielded this indignity from his men. He could hear them, without taking his eyes from the old man's face, slowly creeping closer, crawling on the sand to show a proper humility and to hide their fear.

The witch doctor said: "None of your men will be killed. Now that I have come to help you, none of your men will be killed. You will give me one man, a man who can run fast."

The Captain said promptly: "The son of Obangu."

"And the body of the man Carrierco."

The Captain smiled. "I will kill him for you. Now."

The witch doctor said sharply: "No! I need his living body for my magic."

He turned to Owadi and told him what to do.

Owadi took the ceremonial knife he carried for his master, the witch doctor, tested the edge with his thumbnail, and squatted down happily beside Carrierco.

Carrierco looked up at him and said: "Thank God it's you, Owadi. For a moment I was frightened—you've recruited a lot of savages since I last saw you. Cut me free."

Owadi grinned and said: "We are all savages now." He put down the knife, opened the heavy overcoat, and undid Carrierco's belt.

Carrierco said in sudden alarm: "What are you doin? Cut me free!"

"To tell you the truth," Owadi said, "I thought you'd finish like this one day."

"Finish..."

"You shouldn't have warned M'Butu. How much did you think he'd pay you?"

Carrierco said desperately, the fear rising and quite engulfing him: "Owadi, friend Owadi..."

"He's a wealthy man, more than a thousand cattle, but that won't do him any good now, either."

He was pulling the trousers away from the groin, and when Carrierco began to struggle violently, Owadi called out to one of the other warriors and said sharply: "Hold him!"

Carrierco began to tremble, and then to moan, and then suddenly his violent screams shattered the silence of the night, so piercing that up on the walls of Darhuzuni, the defenders stared out in sudden alarm across the dark, unholy desert.

The witch doctor peered at the son of Obangu, whose name was Jomo, as he stood trembling in the darkness in front of him. (The young man wished there were more than just one fire to drive away the devils that were around this wicked old man, almost visible, and

148

certainly able to be smelled). The skin hung from the witch doctor's bones as though there were no flesh under it at all, hanging in folds that seemed to sway in cadence with his movements. He had once been so fat that six men had had to carry him whenever he wanted to move anywhere, which was rarely, but now the bag was deflated, and the skin was wrinkled and dried out like old leather that has not been properly cared for.

Jomo stared and began to wish he had never left his distant village, never listened to the angry, eager men who had come to his compound with stories of the great uprising on the other side of the mountains.

The witch doctor peered into his eyes and said: "Have I seen you before?"

Jomo trembled. The schools had never succeeded in stifling the fear he felt of the tribal doctors. He said, stammering: "My father...my father is Obangu, who perhaps is known to you. I am...his...his eighth son."

"And the others?" Saliva was slowly spilling, uncontrolled, from the old man's mouth.

"All alive, except one. Three are in the city, working—"

He broke off, dreading the next question. Only in the eyes of the witch doctor was there any life; his face was dead, his limbs were motionless, but there was a deep dark fire in his black eyes, a fire that seemed eager to burst out of the tiny, narrow slits in the parchment face.

"Working? For the white man?"

Jomo wondered if he should lie. He took a deep breath and said: "For the white man. One of them, my oldest brother, killed his boss. He pushed him in the sea when he was drunk. The police thought...they thought it was an accident. He still...he still works there, and one day he will kill another white man." The old man looked at him, not moving, and he said again, desperately: "One day, he wants to kill another white man."

Now the old head gently moved up and down, and a choking sound came from the throat, finally resolving itself into the word *saba*, seven, repeated over and over: *Saba...saba...saba...saba...* It was the magic number.

149

Jomo shuddered.

At last, the witch doctor reached across to Owadi and took from him a bloody tangle of wet skin and muscle and said sharply: "A stick!"

Someone quickly gave him a three-foot length of *mvuli* twig, and with the intestine of a cat which he took from his pouch he slowly bound one end of the wet flesh to the stick, shaking it slowly until it resolved itself into its proper form; it was the penis and scrotum Owadi had cut from Carrierco's living body.

He held it out to Jomo and said: "Take. This will protect you."

Jomo felt a tremor of revulsion run through him. He shook his head and stammered, and said: "But what...what will it protect me from?"

The Captain stepped forward and took the gruesome stick from the old man's trembling hand, and thrust it savagely at Jomo's face.

He said angrily (trying to show the witch doctor he believed him): "Take it! You heard what you were told! Take it!"

Jomo took it from him reluctantly, feeling the slime of it running down the palm of his hand and over the wrist.

He said: "Of course, I take it. But...but I do not understand."

The witch doctor's face twitched, and a shudder went through him. He said angrily: "There is no need for you to understand! When the sun comes up, you will watch, you will watch until the white men go to work on the well, and then you will run forward with a grenade that your leader will give you, and you will drop the grenade in the well. Do you understand *that?*"

The gray in the sky was spreading fast, and now it stood above the broken silhouette of the house. "But in daylight...they will see me. They will kill me."

The witch doctor said gravely: "They will see you, but they will not harm you." He touched the bloody stick with a thin finger and said: "This, the *uchawi* that you do not understand, this will protect you. When they fire their guns, the bullets will turn to water and they will not harm you."

In the silence, Jomo could not control the shivering. He would have expected a murmur of wonder, but there was silence, and this made him believe that perhaps some of the men (gathered now in a silent circle behind him) were also thinking as he was. He took courage from their silence and said: "*Maji-maji?*"

The phrase meant *water-water*, and was the name given to the great rebellion about which he had been told by his father (whose father was killed in it), the rebellion against the white men from the German tribe.

The witch doctors had said the same thing then: "*Do not fear the bullets of the white men, for they will turn to water.*" More than three thousand screaming tribesmen, waving their spears, had charged the thin gray line of the German troops, and more than two thousand of them had been ruthlessly shot down.

The witch doctor's eyes did not leave his face. He nodded slowly and repeated: "The bullets will turn to water."

Jomo, finding more courage, more daring in the silence, said: "I am an educated man, I went to school, I can read. I read in a book once that the German tribe killed many of the Nandi with their water bullets."

It was perhaps the first time that he had been denied. The witch doctor trembled so violently that one of the warriors got to his feet and held his arms to steady him, casting malevolent glances at Jomo.

The old man said at last, his thin voice filled with venom: "The white men taught you only lies. The Nandi killed three hundred of the white men with their spears, and not one warrior died. Not one warrior, because the bullets turned to water. It was so because I say it was so, and all that I do not say is a lie."

"But it is...in the book, the history book, for everyone to read who has learned to read."

The patience came back, because now the witch doctor knew how he would punish the effrontery of this youth. He said slowly, for the benefit of the others: "It is written in a white man's book, and all that is written there is a lie, for a white man gave you the book."

There was no support for him anywhere. Jomo said unhappily: "Yes, a white man..."

"It is a lie."

The old man began to lean back slowly, and quickly one of his bodyguard knelt behind him to be leaned on, supporting the tired old head with his cupped hands. The red-rimmed eyes closed, and his ancient face, like the face of a ghoul, became immobile. The argument was over.

He said again: "When it is light, go and drop your grenade down the well, but wait first until they are working there so that some of them will die with the well."

When Jomo did not move, the Captain said quietly (wondering the while how he could use his military talents to make this operation fruitful): "It will soon be light and they will be working. Go to the top of the tree and watch."

Jomo said: "I am afraid. Afraid of the bullets."

He wanted to put down the loathsome stick with its bloody *uchawi* that smelled of evil, but his courage began to ebb away again.

The Captain looked quickly at the witch doctor, dreading the immobility of the fragile body. The witch doctor opened his eyes again, and suddenly they were alive with fire, burning with hidden fire in the dead face.

He looked at the Captain and said, knowing this was a test of their strengths: "One of my own men will do this thing for you. And I will deal with this one."

He took the *uchawi* stick and handed it to Owadi, and said slowly: "Bring me sand, and a burning branch, and some feathers, and the eyes of the man Carrierco."

One of his own warriors heaped sand into a small earthenware bowl, and another began to shave the root of a eucalyptus branch into a stringy brush, and another of them brought him some feathers, and then Owadi walked softly over to where Carrierco was still lying, moaning slightly, his consciousness coming and going in agonized waves...

A terrible fear came over Jomo, and he wanted to run, but his legs were held to the ground as though long nails had been driven through his feet into the earth; he dropped to his knees, and still his feet would not move. He hardly heard the sudden, violent scream that came from Carrierco.

When Owadi came back he began to sob quietly, and the Captain hit him in the face with his fist and said roughly: "You do not believe all this, an educated man, so why do you cry?"

Soon the brand was ready for burning, and the witch doctor

burned the feathers in its flames, and as the acrid smoke rose up in a blue spiral, he sprinkled sand into the palm of his hands, added some crystals to it (which he took from a small leather pouch at his fleshless waist), and added the sand to the flames and watched the fire burn green for a moment

And then Owadi took Jomo's ears and held them to force his head up, gray now with terror, and the witch doctor took in his skinny fist the two wet eyeballs Owadi had pulled from Carrierco's face, and held them under Jomo's nose, and then he crushed them, and as the juice ran down his bony wrists he said:

"As the sight in my hands is dying, as the eyes can no longer see, so you will die." He repeated: "You will die, you will die..." seven times, and then there was nothing but silence.

Owadi let go of Jomo's head, and he fell forward into the sand; a chip of hard granite was pressing into his cheek, but he could not move to shift it. And then, at last, he got slowly to his feet and stumbled off into the bush, and went away from the others, and sank to the ground and looked up at the stars and at the gray streaks of the east.

For a while, he sat there, his legs spread out before him, his shoulders hunched. His mind was numb, his senses were dazed; an atrophy was slowly settling over him. The air grew cold, but he did not move to bring his cloak closer about his wasted body, and all sound had ceased; his impercipient eyes were glazed.

As the gray in the sky turned to red, and then to yellow, as the bright pale beams began to tell of the heat that was already scalding the ocean out there to the east beyond the edge of the desert, he slowly keeled over onto his side.

The shadow that was all that was left of the night raced across the damp sand, and the desert began to dry up again.

And then, the boy called Jomo, the son of Obangu, shuddered once, and died.

CHAPTER 11

The sun was hardly up before the three of them trooped out of the house, warily, searching the desert and finding nothing.

The night's attack had been a careless, unsuccessful foray against them; they had learned their lesson from it, and they knew that the *watu* would learn one, too, and so they had ranged their defensive forces with infinite care.

Babajee, carrying the long rope, the bucket, and the collapsible shovel, was flanked by Tabor and Willis with their rifles ready. Above them, on the heights of the portico, Bradley had placed a group of a dozen bottles filled with gas, their necks stuffed with pieces of rag; his lighter was ready, and the .306 was beside him. To his right, high on the gable, Marion waited with her Magnum, resting it comfortably on the stonework, crouched down behind it so that only her yellow hair was visible. Far to his left, half-hidden by the ornate but broken curlicues of the old veranda, Petna stood close against the wall, holding the shotgun and waiting fearfully, watching her father below. On the seaward side, M'Butu stood alone, his huge frame wedged in by the chimney.

The sun was pale and bright, low in the sky, but they could already feel the heat of it striking at them, and Babajee ran his tongue over his lips, feeling for any telltale blisters, knowing that in the heat that was coming at them, a day and a half without water could be dangerous.

It was his second day in the well, and the fear of the darkness down there had lessened; not gone entirely, but at least receded. He knew a fierce feeling of pride, and he wanted to say (but did not): "You see? You cannot manage without me."

Willis said to him gravely: "Carrierco will have told them how badly we need water, Baba, and they might try to rush us. If they do..." He gestured vaguely, and said: "What do you want us to do? To bring you up, or leave you down there? The bottom of the well might just be the safest place."

Babajee thought about it for a while and said: "Whatever you think is best, really..."

Tabor said: "I agree, down there you'll be safer. We start pulling you up during an attack, some bright boy's going to take a bead on the top of the well and wait for your head to come up. We can keep them out of rifle range with good shooting, but...if too many of them come at us at once, one or two might slip through. But it's up to you, whatever you want."

Babajee said carefully: "I do not think that any attack will succeed in getting close enough to the well if you are all firing. And, to tell the truth, I would be happier if I knew that every gun was firing, that no one was occupied in pulling me up, don't you think?"

"That's exactly what I think," Willis said.

Babajee stared down into the well and said, making a joke of it: "Today I will find you enough water to float Mr. Tabor's raft on. You will see, I feel it in my bones."

"We're all depending on you, Baba," Tabor said. "It's up to you."

Babajee beamed. He said: "Did you know M'Butu gave my daughter his water ration? She did not want to take it, but he made her. Did you know that?"

"Yes, I know."

For the last two hours, Tabor had been teaching Petna to load and reload the shotgun quickly till at last he had said: "You see? There's nothing to it, you're as fast as I am."

Looking up at her now, Babajee could not hide the shame he felt, but he tried. He said ponderously: "We are not a fighting people, Mr. Willis, and look up there at my daughter..."

"She's a good girl." Willis smiled and said gently: "We can count on her, too, if we have to. I hope we won't."

"In my country, as you must know, we have a special tribe who do our fighting for us. But I am not sure, really, that this is a more civilized approach to the perplexing question of man's interrelationship with man."

Tabor said cheerfully: "Over you go, Baba, and find us some water."

Babajee looked back once at Petna, regretfully, sorrowing for the dejection he knew was on her, as his fingers automatically explored the security of the knot in the rope that encircled his narrow body. Then he stood over the edge of the well. He looked at Tabor, who stood ready to lower him, and saw with surprise that Tabor was grinning at him.

"You're all right, Baba," the American said. "When this is over I'd like to buy you a drink."

A sudden pleasure suffused his face, and he nodded back, his eyes shining, and then the narrow confines of the shaft began to swallow him up, stifling him, darkening his space; and the round patch of daylight above him grew slowly smaller and more remote.

When he reached the bottom, he freed himself from the rope and stripped off his clothes again. He placed them, neatly folded, on the stone projection, and summoned the energy to put his naked body feverishly to work. Each time he waited for the returning bucket he leaned against the hard, rough sandstone and the broken logs, panting, worrying, knowing that the sweat had stopped coming and that this could mean danger. And then he began to wonder about his daughter and Willis.

All the moisture had gone from his body, and he could feel the weariness numbing him. And then, suddenly, there was water at his feet.

It was a puddle, no more, but he dropped to his knees and scraped at it desperately with his fingers, and then he put his mouth to the wet sand and sucked, and it was sweet and cool to his swollen lips.

He stood up and tried to shout out, but he began to cry instead, and then the patch of light above him was obscured as Tabor leaned over and called down: "Are you all right? Baba, did you say

156

something?"

He brushed away the tears from his face and called up eagerly: "I have found it, there is water!"

"Good work! How is it?"

"It is good, Mr. Tabor, good water..." He filled the bucket quickly, the sand weighing more now and the puddle at his feet growing wider.

When Tabor pulled it up and tipped it out onto the pile, Willis came over and kicked at it and said happily: "Wet sand, we're there, he's made it. Another five or six buckets."

And then, suddenly, they came. It was midday.

Though they were expecting the attack, the surprise that was in the strength of it filled them with dismay. Three hundred yards away, forty or fifty of the rate broke cover all at once, racing across the scrub towards them, waving their spears and their *pangas*, and at the same time a ragged volley of fire broke out from the distant rocks.

Willis said briefly: "Come on!"

And with Tabor beside him he ran forward to the broken wall of the compound. He heard Marion, up on the roof, start shooting, and he saw a tall Kikuyu, two hundred and fifty yards away, twist around and fall, and then he sighted his rifle and methodically began to fire. He heard Bradley's .306 and knew that he was firing too fast for accuracy, and when he looked around to shout a warning he was astonished to see that Petna had left her place and was climbing down the outside of the house, in full view, the shotgun slung over her shoulder, climbing down lithely and quickly from the broken veranda to the architrave over the lower window, and then with a long jump down to the ground.

He stared at her in surprise as she raced across to the well, calling out; "Baba...Baba..." and he shouted at her: "Get back, Petna, get back...!"

The guns were firing fast, and he ran towards her and took her by the shoulders and dragged her away and fought with her as she struggled against him, screaming, and then he heard Tabor yell: "Under cover, everybody!"

He looked back and saw that they were close now, more than thirty of them, and a spear thudded into the timbers of the house, and he dragged Petna towards the door and flung it open and pushed her inside and stood close by it, firing fast as they came nearer, not stopping, and then Tabor was beside him, heading inside and for the window as a shower of spears came at them; he looked down stupidly at his thigh and saw an arrow hanging there, and then Tabor grabbed him and pulled him inside and slammed the door shut, and he fell to the ground and pulled at the arrow, and when it came out he quickly unsheathed his hunting knife and slashed at the wound methodically in crisscross cuts, hard and deep, and then pounded at it to make the blood flow faster...

A sudden faintness came over him, and he fell back, and Petna was suddenly close by him, screaming no longer but ripping the cloth of his trousers away and putting her lips to his leg, sucking out the poison. He struggled to get to his feet, but he could not, and he dragged himself to the window while Petna tugged at his leg, and he propped himself up in the embrasure and began firing again.

A tall Somali, who had joined the *watu* because he hated all white men (twenty years before, the Italians had dropped his father out of an aircraft to teach his tribe a lesson), stood up close by the broken wall and wound his sling around his head in a whistling arc; when he let go of the plaited gut string, it cracked like a rifle, and the stone, the size of a large apricot, flew through the air with incredible force and crashed into the wall behind them. A second stone hit Tabor in the shoulder and sent him spinning to the ground in pain, and Willis fired quickly and saw the Somali fall, and then Tabor was back at the window again, firing fast...

A short, heavily built Kikuyu was running along the wall, looking for a vantage point, and a beer bottle full of flaming gasoline, thrown by Bradley from the roof, hit him in the face and burst into flames, and he ran screaming away, still dragging his rifle after him...

A spear missed Willis' head by an inch, and he heard Tabor fire and say, quite calmly: "That's the last spear he'll ever throw."

Petna was pulling at his trousers, and he thrust her away and said angrily: "Leave it, I'm all right."

He tried to stand up but fell to the floor again, and he swore and tugged at the flask in his pocket and pushed Petna's head away and poured gin into the wound, feeling the searing pain of it, and when he looked out of the window again the *watu* had fallen back, and the ground was littered with their dead; wherever he looked, there were the black shadows of bleeding men on the hard sand, and the living were searching for cover among the scattered bushes. He heard an angry voice in the distance, urging them on, but the compound was empty, save for three of their dead; one of them was still burning.

He saw a thin Kikuyu crawling to cover, his rifle in his hand, and he fired quickly and blew the gun out of his hands and heard the scream as the bullet plowed into the kneecap and shattered it. He saw two more running for cover, but the faintness came again before he could shoot. He shook his head savagely to clear it, and saw that Petna was still beside him, her face white with fear for him as she groped at his wounded leg.

And then a new danger appeared.

The warrior whose name was Owadi came racing across the desert towards them. In one hand, held out in front of him, like a banner, he carried a short stick with a red and shining mass of muscle and skin at the end of it, and in the other, clutched tightly to his bare chest, there were two black spheres that were grenades; their pins were out.

Tabor looked at him and growled: "What the hell does he think he's going to do?" and shot him neatly in the chest. But Owadi did not stop.

And now Willis, too, his head clearing, saw the grenades and fired quickly, twice in rapid succession. His first shot went wild with a burst of sudden blindness, but the sight came back instantly and the second shot took Owadi in the neck, and still he came running. Willis raised his rifle to fire again, swearing now, but the dizziness came again and he crashed back to the floor, and he lay there and shouted: "The head, Tabor, take him in the head..."

Then the nausea of the coma hit him and the world was black.

Deep in the dark well, staring up at the daylight, Babajee listened to the sound of the battle above him, alone in his private world, one hand to his mouth, plucking at his lips. He was thinking: One of them will come down the rope with a naked *panga* in his hand,

and here, in prehistoric darkness, we shall fight. Or shall we? Or will I instead expose my throat to his blade and hope that it is quick?

There was a terrible loneliness on him, and then he thought: They are all good men up there, and they will not let the *watu* get near the well.

Owadi's chest was pockmarked with little dark holes out of which the blood spurted, in precise coordination, it seemed, with the piston movements of his fast-moving feet. He kept running, like a jackrabbit that does not stop nor falter in its speed even after the hunter's bullet had torn out its heart.

The sand leaped up under his flying feet, and as he leaped the low protective wall, Marion's fourth or fifth shot to hit him tore into his shoulder and plowed out again at his belly, and still he clutched his *uchawi* and his grenades. A closer shot from Tabor, livid now with rage and frustration, tore out his throat, and he fell against the low surround of the well, spun around once, and then Tabor's last shot took the top of his head right off. But it was too late; the *uchawi* had done its work.

The empty body was lifeless, had long been so. The flesh and the nerves were held by a power that no man could understand, a power that the white man (if he had never met it) would laugh at, which he would call, with a shrug, *possession*, or *mesmerism*, and then dismiss without a thought because these things lay outside the sphere of his own essentially practical knowledge. It cannot be proved, he would say, and therefore it is not true.

But for Owadi, the truth was there till his work was done. The body swayed, and it hung for a moment over the well, and then it toppled slowly into the shaft.

Fifty feet below, Babajee saw Owadi, no longer a man, falling towards him. He dropped to his knees and covered his face in horror, feeling his nakedness, and when the body hit the sand beside him he trembled at the sudden shock of it.

He looked in dismay at the two grenades, and then they went off and lifted the world of sand that was about him, his private world which the others could not reach, and when the white-hot pieces of metal plowed into his body, he did not feel them, nor did he feel the impact as the earth went up in a violent vacuum and then caved in all around him. He tried to shout his daughter's name, but he was dead before the sound left his lips.

And then, with a monstrous rumbling sound, all that was left of the well, laboriously dug many years ago by the Somalis from over the border, slowly settled back into place, till a shallow depression in the surface of the and desert was all that was left of it, and once more the earth was shrouded with silence.

The *watu* pulled back and began to lick their wounds, and the witch doctor said triumphantly, his evil eyes gleaming: "They are dying."

The Captain was binding a rag round his face, trying to contain the bleeding left by a ricocheting bullet. He said coldly: "We killed one man, and only an Asian. We lost over twenty."

The witch doctor said again: "They are dying. There is no more water. And the hunter...he is already dead. Now you may kill the man Carrierco. We shall not need him again."

But Willis did not die.

The miracle of medicine was too much for the magic of the *uchawi*. Petna had sucked out the deadly strychnine, the alcohol had cauterized the wound, and sulfanilamide had done the rest.

As he lay on the floor and consciousness came back to him, he looked at Petna and saw that she was weeping, her hands over her face; she was crouched on the ground beside him as though in prayer, moaning softly.

Tabor had left the window and was tightly binding the upper part of his thigh with a bandage, and he said slowly, looking at Petna and then away again: "We were wrong, Willis. The well was not the safest place to be in." When Willis stared at him, not understanding, he said: "They got to the well, they dropped a hand grenade down it."

Willis rolled over onto his side and clutched at Petna, and pulled her close to him, conscious that Bradley, standing by the window now, was watching. He said softly: "Don't cry, my darling."

She put her arms tight around him and buried her face in his shoulder.

In a little while, he said quietly to Tabor: "We must have been

161

hit hard."

"Marion, Bradley, Petna, and myself... No damage."

"M'Butu?"

"A broken arm. A slingshot hit him, broke his elbow. Marion's up there with him now, trying to fix it. How do you feel?"

Willis said weakly: "I'm all right."

"I don't know much about this poison they use..."

"It's quick. If you don't die at once, you're going to live. A bit weak, but all right."

"They might come at us again soon."

"And they might give up now. We did a lot of damage."

"A hell of a lot of damage."

"Ammunition?"

"We used a lot, but there's plenty left. It's only the water."

"We've got to get out. The raft?"

Tabor gestured at the lashed spars in the center of the room. He said sourly: "It might float, if we could get it down to the beach, but I won't guarantee it. Some of that wood's pretty rotten."

Bradley looked at Petna for a while, then turned to Tabor and said quietly: "I took a good look at the bodies out there."

"And?"

"Three of them are in some sort of uniform."

"I noticed."

Willis looked up sharply.

Bradley said: "Three of them have water bottles on their belts. I'm going out to get them. You want to cover me? I told Marion, and she's ready, too."

Tabor said: "Maybe you'd better let me go."

Bradley scowled at him and said unpleasantly: "Don't kid yourself you've got a monopoly on guts, Tabor. I'm going out to get them."

He put aside his rifle and went to the door, flung it open, and stood there looking out across the desert for a moment; and then he ran for the wall, leaped lightly over it, and raced across the scrub. Tabor stood at the window, his rifle ready, and waited.

Not a shot was fired. In a few moments, Bradley came back, panting hard, and handed over three water bottles without a word.

162

Tabor took them, put his lips to each one in turn, and said: "It seems all right. A touch of gypsum, maybe, but it's good." He looked at Bradley and smiled. He said softly: "Good work. Enough to last us for another three days."

Bradley said nothing. He looked at Petna again and his face was white, but he did not go to her. Instead, he turned on his heel and went quickly up the stairs.

CHAPTER 12

"Come down, M'Butu!" Tabor called. "Come down and sleep!"

He swung himself up over the last rafter and rolled over on his stomach on the tiles, looking down at the sea that gently rolled three hundred feet below, deep down at the bottom of the sheer drop to the tiny beach, perilously far away.

When M'Butu did not answer, he crawled carefully along the steep slope of the roof, digging his toes in, feeling the hazardous motion of the laths under his weight, and when he reached the old man he said again: "Come down and get some sleep. I'll watch up here."

The huge brown hand was curled upwards, lying in the lap formed by the robe M'Butu wore around his waist, the fingers pointing skyward, seeming to stiffen.

Tabor looked at it and said: "Flex your fingers, old man, let me see you flex them."

M'Butu grinned at him, but his eyes were heavy with pain. He said: "A Somali slingshot, a Somali! All my life I have tried not to hate any man, but to tell the truth, the Somalis make it very difficult for me. I would have almost welcomed a spear from an honest-to-God African, but a Somali!" He leaned back against the chimney and said: "And Willis? And yourself?"

"Willis is all right now. And my arm, I'd forgotten about it." The white bandage was stained yellow with the powder and red with his blood, and he said: "Just a bunch of bloody cripples. But I can still use it well enough."

M'Butu raised his rifle to his shoulder with his right arm and said: "Yes, and so can I. You see how good my God is? He gave me two arms so that I could still shoot straight even when a bedeviled Somali had broken one of them." His face was twisted with pain, and his eyes were grave. He said softly: "I think we are losing this battle."

Tabor shook his head. "Not on your life. One more charge like that and we'll break the back of it. They've got to learn, sooner or later, they've got to."

M'Butu ignored the protest. He was watching Tabor closely. He said: "And I am the man who brought them to this house."

"What's that supposed to mean?"

"It means that if I had run elsewhere, perhaps they would not have come here to kill you. It is *my* body they want to run their spears through."

"Oh? Then what about the passengers on the bus?"

"The Indian, Babajee. They hate the Indians too."

"And not us? Is that what you want to say?"

M'Butu said slowly, raising a finger at him: "The white man's rule in Africa has always been based on undeniable logic, and therefore no one has ever thought to dispute it. But now, now that the white man himself is beginning to question it—and can you tell me why he should?—then the African is merely doing just the same thing, just like the men he has always followed, always relied upon to tell him what to do. But you, *Bwana* Tabor, you do not question, do you?"

"I believe I'm a better man than any of that bunch out there, if that's what you mean, and so are you. That's a kind of logic I won't try to deny."

M'Butu shrugged. "For me...these are my descending years, and once the descent has started it is hard to move up again. But for you..."

"Just what are you getting at, M'Butu?"

"I believe that if you went out there and spoke to them...not *pleaded* with them, but *ordered* them...I think perhaps they would obey you."

Tabor said: "You're looking for common sense in your own people, and I'm not so sure you'll find it there. There's no common ground we could argue on."

"Not argue. Tell."

Tabor sighed. "I'd like to think you were right, but I know damn well you're not."

M'Butu made a hopeless gesture. "Perhaps."

There were blisters on the old man's tips, and Tabor said sharply: "When did you last drink?"

"I do not need water. I am a camel."

"I think you'd better take your ration anyway."

M'Butu said slowly: "Perhaps if I were to give myself to them...do you think they would go away?"

"No. I don't think that. I think they'll try and kill every one of us."

"You cannot be sure."

"Sure enough. I just can't see them parting their ranks and letting us walk through them... Yes, I'm sure, so there's no use talking like that, okay?"

A slow smile spread over M'Butu's flabby face, and his eyes wrinkled. "Good, Mr. Tabor, good. I would not like to think that you expected me to give myself up in an effort to save you that could not, I think, possibly succeed. But I wanted to know...if perhaps you had been thinking like this."

Tabor was watching him closely, wishing he could understand more clearly what went on in that shrewd mind. Willis had said: *We'll never begin to understand them. Just when you think you know what they're going to do...*

He said: "If I thought they wanted you, and you only, then maybe I'd start worrying about the women, worrying if we ought to give you to them; does that make you happy? But I don't believe that. I know they want all of us, and we'll all get out of here together, so the hell with that kind of talk."

"Inside my brain," M'Butu said, "the thought has been worrying at me, like a leopard trying to find its way out of a trap..."

"You and Carrierco both," Tabor said, "you haven't got the brains of a warthog between you. Now, go on down and get some sleep."

M'Butu shook his head. "When I came up here, I swore to

166

myself that I would never come down until the battle was over." He said slyly: "You think it is easy for me, for a man with a waist like mine? To climb down again? I will sleep here where it is safe and comfortable, where I can look at the stars and thank my gods for sending me such good friends."

Tabor looked at him curiously: "You've known Willis a long time."

"For more than forty years. The life-span of a man. I would give my life for him, and he would do the same for me. Is that an old-fashioned idea?"

"Perhaps. But I like it better than...than the new idea out there." He jerked his thumb towards the desert and said: "What is it they really want, M'Butu, can you tell me that? What the hell can they hope to achieve?"

"What does a leopard want when he breaks through a *zeriba* and kills every animal he can find? Why does a leopard, like man himself, kill wantonly, without reason?"

"You tell me."

"How can I know such a thing," M'Butu asked, "when they do not even know themselves? If you put a firebrand in the hand of a child, it is no good asking: 'Why do you burn down the house, my son?' And this is all they are doing; they are burning down the house that your people tried to build for them."

"And there's nothing we can do to stop it?"

"Nothing."

Tabor looked out across the scrub, white under the bright moon. He said: "And out there, nothing's moving. Nothing."

"No, Mr. Tabor," M'Butu said slowly. "Out there, there is a movement. It is slow, inexorable, and it started many years ago, many, many years ago. It is a movement of sadness."

Tabor said impatiently: "How the hell can you find compassion for those people? There's no sadness there, there's nothing but hate in their hearts and confusion in their minds."

"No, not that. The *watu* are just another group of terrorists, of no consequence to anyone save for one thing—that because of them, we might all die. But the movement that is out there gave rise to the *watu* as it gave rise to the politicians who are trying to twist their sad

167

thinking to fit their own distorted causes. And that is a movement that was started by the white people themselves. Will you say that the military might of the white men cannot put a stop to the rampaging of a few hundred fanatics? Of course not! And I will tell you why. It is because the white man's great weakness is that he wallows in self-accusation and has become his own worst enemy; it is because of men like Bradley who say: 'I have used you cruelly, and therefore you must flagellate me.' But my people have not been used cruelly, Mr. Tabor; my people have been used well, only..."

"Only what?"

"Once," M'Butu said, "I was a great chief, a leader of all my tribe. When I was a young man, I was a King, and in my tribe there was never any trouble. If the young men got out of hand, when their passions ran wild and the evil that is in all men was allowed to show itself, the white men—they were the German tribe then—bound them to whipping posts in the public squares and beat them, and there was no more evil, for this my young men fully understood, that evil must be rewarded with pain. But then the British came, and they stopped the whippings and the young men knew that they could do what they wanted and they would not be punished. The British stopped the tribal wars, too, and so there was no longer any need for my young men to be strong, and thus they became weak. And the British took away the authority that was in the elders of the tribes and they said: 'All the respect you learned in your youth for the tribal wisemen is a lie, for all men, good or bad, wise or foolish, are equal...' And this was the great lie that was the beginning of the movement that is taking place out there now. It is a movement downhill and there is no stopping it."

When Tabor did not speak, M'Butu looked at him for a while, envying his assurance, and said slowly: "I have been left in a vacuum, Mr. Tabor. I reached the height of my life as a young man, and ever since, the power has been slowly stripped away from me until, at an age when a man should have earned himself the maximum of respect, I am left with nothing. My name is Paramount Chief Juma Onyanga Mchrubi M'Butu, and the name is hollow, like an empty gourd from which the water has been drained. For a long time I have known this; but perhaps now, as I sit here on a deserted rooftop, with an arm broken by a wretched Somali's slingshot, I am realizing for the first time that the white men have made me a shadow; and they have done it through kindness. Perhaps it would have been better if they had merely killed me when I was in my prime."

He pulled the broken arm around slowly and looked at the bandage over it and said: "The power I once had, which could have stopped this rampaging of my people with a word, has been broken, as my arm has been broken. My life has been wasted, and all that is left for me is to find a chief's honor in death."

"Nobody's going to die," Tabor said, "not anymore. We've broken their back. Now get some sleep."

The Captain's head was giving him trouble. The blood-soaked bandage had stifled the bleeding, but the lead of the bullet was working its poison, and his cheek had swollen to horrible proportions. He had made a pulp of *mchufa* leaves and was holding the mass of it over the wound, his stolid eyes open wide as if they were quite unfeeling, as though the pain that shot through his head in tiny arrows of anguish were not there at all. He was watching the black silhouette of Darhuzuni, stark and silent against the evening sky, and waiting, lying on a blanket that had been thrown down on the sand for him by the young woman from the bus.

Close beside him, one of the warriors from a village near Mwadi was crouched on his heels, his long fingers dangling between his knees, telling the Captain something he thought he ought to know. His name was Osale Mongo.

Drawing a thin finger across the sand, he was saying: "Here, to the west of the house, a small valley."

The Captain slewed around painfully and watched the tracing fingers.

Osale said: "I went there unseen with three men, and the valley is as deep as the length of a tall man's leg, and as wide as the compound of a man's hut, and before it comes to a stop on the cliff above the water, it passes close to the wall of Darhuzuni."

The Captain said sharply: "How close?"

"As far as a child can throw a small stone."

"Fifty paces?"

169

Osale thought for a long time, wishing he had not been asked to be so explicit. He said at last, again: "As far as a child can throw a small stone."

"And how many men can hide in it?"

"Four, perhaps five, if they do not wish to be seen."

"Can you throw a spear from the valley to reach the door of the house?"

"The door, no, because the door is too far away. But I can throw a spear to reach the wall. This is where the white woman with the big gun was hiding before we began the attack. Then she moved to the front of the house and I could not have reached her."

"And a man with a bow?"

Osale said scornfully: "I do not use the bow, I am a spearman."

The Captain insisted: "But if I sent there a man with a bow as well?"

"He could shoot his arrows over the wall and into the house through the windows."

"A pity you did not tell me of this earlier, Osale. Now, the night has come."

"And only at night can the valley be reached."

"You should have told me earlier."

"Earlier, you were with your friend."

When Osale said "your friend" the Captain knew that he was terrified of the witch doctor.

"And can a man reach this valley without being seen?"

Osale shrugged. "I reached it during the battle, when the white men were busy at the front of the house."

The Captain looked up at the sky, growing gray with incredible speed.

He said to Osale: "You know my son, the young man named Mwipi?"

"I know him."

"Send him to me. And send me also six of the best warriors."

Osale waited for a while to show that when he moved he did so of his own volition, and not because he was ordered to do so, and then he got up slowly, picked a thorn out of his foot with the point of his spear, and went off to find Mwipi.

170

He was a handsome young man, Mwipi, the Captain's favorite son, just past his seventeenth birthday, though he did not know this. (When the District Officer had once asked the Captain: 'How old is your son Mwipi?' he had answered scornfully: 'Is he a cow that I should know his age?')

He was tall and straight-limbed, and some said that the blood of a Somali or a Watusi flowed in his veins, though none would say this to his father. He had spent all his life by his father's side, fighting with him, learning from him, caring for him, and he did not like the desert here; he remembered the lush green forests of his home, far to the north; but his father's duty was among these simple peasants and that was where Mwipi wanted to be, as always, with the man he admired and tried to emulate.

He came at Osale's bidding and sat cross-legged on the sand close to his father, and looked at his swollen face and grinned, and said: "Now you look more than ever like a warrior."

His father sat up and threw aside the blanket and said: "I *am* a warrior, and the time is coming to fight again."

The other men began drifting in, moving without noise as though the coming night were infecting them with its silence, moving on bare feet that were splayed over the sand like the feet of camels. Some of them sat down and waited, and some of them just stood there, fingering their weapons and looking stolidly at the Captain.

He wished he could know what they were thinking, and he said, almost angrily: "Enough! We have been playing with these people for long enough. Now, we will kill them."

Osale, one of the six himself (the Captain had said 'the best warriors...'), had sliced a great gash in his foot to remove the thorn, and now he was rubbing wood-ash into the wound.

He said carefully, not wanting to offend the Captain: "It is not playing when they have killed so many of us."

The Captain said, keeping his temper: "At first there were nine of them, and now there are only six. Tonight, two of you will enter the house of Darhuzuni, silently, in the darkness, and there you will kill them all."

In the silence, Mwipi laughed suddenly and said: "Not the white woman, she must not be killed."

171

The Captain turned and looked at him and put out a hand and held it on his black curly head, and he said softly: "If that is what you want, my son, that is what you will have. I will give her to you myself."

Osale said: "I saw her too, and I would rather cut off her breasts than lie with her. She is too thin for much pleasure."

The Captain did not take his hand away from his son's head. He said proudly: "My son will be one of the two, and he will have the white woman, no one else until he has finished with her. The others of you can have the Indian girl, and for myself..." He looked into the distance, seeming to project his thoughts there, and said: "I want the heads of the three white men."

"And M'Butu?"

The Captain looked at Osale and said quietly: "I do not care what happens to M'Butu. If you want to kill him, do so. If not, let him go, it is all the same to me."

Osale said: "Many of us went to Mwadi especially to kill him. We went there because he was trying to raise his people against us and it was right to kill him. And because of this, many of us have died. And now you say let him go."

The Captain said patiently: "I do not say that. I say that I do not care what happens to him. For me, the enemy is the white man."

"M'Butu is the friend of the white man."

"Then kill him. What do I care?" The Captain shrugged broadly and said: "It is known, Osale, that you want to take M'Butu's cassava field, but do not bring your personal hatreds to me and say that I must be interested in them. I say kill him, or do not kill him, it is all the same."

"I want his blood, not his fields."

The Captain looked at him curiously and said, as though he had only just remembered it: "Of course, your ceremonies. If you think the blood of a fat old man who is a weakling, a coward, a cheat, and a liar can make you strong, then drink it. I do not care."

The other men, some of the diehards among them, growled and began to mutter among themselves, and the Captain said sharply: "So kill him, it is all the same to me, drink his blood, but for me...my god is here!" He clutched his rifle from the sand and held it up and shook it at them and said fiercely: "This is my god, and with this I will conquer all my enemies!"

One of the six who was a Muslim said shortly: "They are all nonbelievers, and their blood is unclean. Better to make sport with them and let their blood flow into the sand. But tell us how we can get into the house of Darhuzuni, when there are six rifles guarding it."

The Captain was glad to change the subject to one he understood better. He pointed in the direction Osale had shown him and said: "When it is dark, a few of us will go to a *wadi*, a small gulley which runs close by the house at the side, and from there two of you will enter the house without being seen. If you fail in what you have to do, you will come back to the *wadi* and there we will all wait until it is light, and then we will charge them again, but this time from a distance of only fifty paces. Some of us will die, but this will be the last time, because when we have finished, none of them will be alive."

Mwipi laughed again and said: "Except the women."

The Captain patted him on the cheek and said: "Except the women. Enjoy her, my son. Enjoy her well so that I will be pleased for you." He took the long bow from Mwipi's hand, the long Ethiopian bow that Mwipi had taken in a tribal raid three years before, and said softly: "In the house, you will use only bows, and spears, and *pangas*. There must be no shooting, because they will be scattered all over the house and they must be found one by one and killed silently so that the others will not know. My son will be one of those who enter, and Osale will be the other. I will lead the group that stays in support. Maboka Kumburu will take charge of the rest of my men here."

"Good," said Mwipi.

The Captain said: "There is a place at the side of the house where you can climb to the veranda on the upper floor. But I think the stones are loose, you must take care."

Osale's face began to light up.

"We have a good man to lead us, and tonight all the white men will be killed!"

One of the six warriors, laughing too, began to beat on a small wooden drum, his eyes shining, and soon the others were crowding around him, stomping their feet and shuffling around in the sand, and the man with the drum began to sing in a high, nasal tone, improvising the verse as he went along:

"Tonight we shall strike,
Like the lion in the night,
And a brave man shall lead us,
A brave man, a brave man..."

The thin, reedy voice carried far, and on the walls of the big house the defenders stood watching anxiously, listening, worrying, knowing that the drum and the singing would give the attackers courage.

Willis said briefly: "They'll be coming soon now. We'd better get ready for them."

Marion had slipped a pull-through down the barrel of her rifle. She held it up to the fading light and squinted down it and said: "A gallon of boiling water, that's what this needs."

There was only a bottle and a half left now, and they were already beginning to feel the warning dryness of the skin, the lack of perspiration which is the first sign of dehydration.

She said irritably: "And a good double Scotch is what I need."

Tabor drove a spike into a crossbeam of his raft and stepped back to look at it. The spars had been fastened together with spikes he had driven into holes burned with a red-hot bolt, and the empty gasoline cans had been strapped into place underneath it and fastened there with strips of canvas taken from the seats of the Land Rover. When Marion had said, curiously: "Why don't you use the rope?" he had jerked his head at the long coil that lay in the center of the room and had said:

"It's as long as half the height of the cliff. We'll need every inch of it and a lot more if we're ever going to get down to the water."

She had said: "You really think we can, don't you?"

"Yep."

Now, he looked at the crude raft and growled: "You think that's going to float?" He looked at Marion with a quick grin and said: "And if you want a drink there's a full bottle of gin. A couple of slugs won't hurt you."

She sighed and turned away to hide her frustration. "No, we'd better hang on to it, we might have a better use for it." He could feel the edge to her voice, and when she caught him throwing a quick glance at Willis she laughed suddenly and said: "Besides, it's liable to make a loose woman tight."

Nobody laughed with her; the death of Babajee hung like a pall over them, and she suddenly shuddered and said: "Nothing but death in the air, what a hell of a country."

Tabor said: "Grab hold of that spar for me, hold it tight."

She put down her gun and pulled the old rafter into position for him while he hammered in a bolt he had heated to white-hot brilliance over a tiny fire of thorn twigs.

When the sizzling smoke had died down, he pulled it out and examined the hole he had made and said: "We'll all be out of here in time, so let's not worry too much."

She said again: "Nothing but death. Last night, I lay awake thinking, trying to persuade myself about...about repentance, does that seem silly?"

Tabor said dryly: "There's nothing duller than repentance. Or less rewarding."

"Yes, I know. And yet...when it's dark, and silent...I'm scared stiff that some bloody god I don't believe in is going to reach down and pluck at me because of something I did ten years ago, pick me up like a chicken and wring my neck. I don't believe in him, and yet he frightens me. Shows what your inhibitions really are, doesn't it? The Stone Age creeping through and telling us what our ancestors were like. Just like...*theirs*."

Bradley, in the big empty room that was at the north end of the house on the upper floor, was standing at the window watching the darkness descend on the desert. The moon was bright, and the change of light was from yellow to a kind of luminescent glow that made him think of phosphorus in the water. The darkness was in the hills that he could still see far away on the horizon, but a white gleam was over the desert, a ghostly gleam that was almost tangible. He looked at his watch and wondered how long it would be before the beautiful moon went down, abandoning them to the terrors of the darkness.

He was miles away, thinking of the water in the river at home, in some rain-swept little provincial town, and he started in sudden shock when he found Petna beside him. He had not heard her come, and his throat was suddenly dry. *If I do not hear her*, he thought, *will I ever hear them?*

She was smiling at him, but her face was white and anxious. She held out a cigarette for him silently, and when he took it she held a match for him; her hand was trembling, and the flame lit the soft lines of her face, caught the reflections in her huge brown eyes, and cast the shadow of her cheekbones across them so that they looked slanted, almost oriental in their brilliance.

Then the match went out and she said softly: "Willis told me to come and sit with you for a while."

He frowned. "Willis did that?"

"Yes, Willis."

His mouth twitched at the corners, and he looked at her and said: "What the hell's he trying to prove?" He said bitterly: "Crumbs from the rich man's table."

He felt her exploring hand reach for his and grip it tightly, and she said: "He only wants us to be together for a while."

"I saw the way you and he..." He swung around on her angrily and said: "For God's sake, was that just a sudden passion, or has this been going on for...for God's sake, how long?"

"A long time."

"I might have known! It takes a thing like this to...to bring home the truth."

He turned away, trembling with anger, and she said gently: "We have been lovers for a long time, long before..." It was hard to put it into words, and when he looked at her almost in shock, she looked away and said: "I even told him once, that I would go to him, if he wanted me, after I had married you."

The anger was driving away his lucidity and he began to stammer: "And yet...you... you tell me...you have the gall to tell me that you love me? And he has the gall to...for Christ's sake, to send you to me? Just who the hell does he think he is?"

"He sends me to you because he knows."

"Knows what, for God's sake?"

"He knows that we won't come out of this alive. He is trying to hide what he knows, but I understand him, understand the secret thoughts..."

"I'll bet you do."

For a moment, she did not move, and then she let go of his hand and made as if to step back, and he reached for her urgently and said: "No, don't go. I'm...I'm sorry, I didn't mean that. It's just...a bit of a shock, that's all. So many things I believed in... All at once...they all come to nothing. Nothing."

He put an arm around her waist and pulled her close to him, and together they stared out into the bright, silent night, just the two of them alone in a forgotten world where all the evil was hidden, still waiting but out of sight and therefore easy to ignore as long as they could force themselves to feel that there was nothing around them but the aura of their love.

He said slowly: "As far as you can project your thoughts, and then as far again, and as far again, there is nothing. Out there, in a straight line, Juba, Tana, Naivasha, Buganda, Mabode, Ababua, Ubangi, Chad...you've gone two thousand miles and where are you? You're still in the middle of...of nothing. You could walk in a straight line for six months, for a year, and you'd see nothing but...desert, and scrub, and jungle, and...emptiness. There are European towns within a couple of hundred miles of us, and what are they? Little groups of lost people, and all around them is nothing but emptiness."

He could feel the sadness on her. He said gently: "But I don't care what Willis thinks. This is the third night we've been here, and I don't believe...I don't know, someone's bound to find us, sooner or later."

She said gently: "Someone? Who?"

It was hard to contain his anger. He said furiously: "I don't know who! Somebody! I just know we can't be pinned down like this indefinitely, without *somebody* finding out about it! There's a couple of hundred naked savages out there, armed to the bloody teeth, you think someone isn't going to notice *that?* Sooner or later?"

"Only..."

"Only what, for Christ's sake?"

"A man can walk for ten, fifteen days in this part of the world and see nobody. You said so yourself. Sometimes, I go with my father..." She was almost crying, stifling the tears. She checked herself and said: "Sometimes, we used to drive to the villages, you know, to find skins, and incense, and honey... Sometimes, we would see nobody, even driving a truck, for a week at a time. Nobody." She put both her hands on his chest, and laid her head close to them, feeling the heartbeat.

He said slowly: "I've done a lot of foolish things in my time, I suppose, and one thing makes up for all of them. I fell in love with a wonderful woman."

"He wanted us...so badly...to get married."

For a while he held his arms around her, saying nothing, and then he bent down and kissed her and said: "You know how much I've wanted it. Was it...I wondered always why you'd never tell me when... Was it because of Willis?"

"Yes."

"But you don't truly love him."

She could not meet his eyes. "I don't know. Can a woman not love...two men at the same time?"

Bradley said, muttering: "And now, he...he *sends* you to me. Is he so sure of himself, is that it? Or has he given you up?" He could not hide the bitter frustration.

She turned to look at him and said gently: "Or has he given up hope for all of us? Is it because he knows there is not much time left for any of us?"

"If Willis thought that, he'd take you himself, not pass you magnanimously over to me. That's the kind of man Willis is. The king of the bloody jungle, loading it over all of us."

"No!" Forcing the desperation away from her, she said: "I know him well...better than you do! He knows that the end is very close, for all of us, and he is trying to... He will not say so, but I understand what he is trying to do. He is trying so hard to make up for the hurt he has caused us both. And he does that because he knows that there is no time left for anything but...but repentance."

"For God's sake...!"

She insisted. "He knows! The water is nearly finished, and there is no way out for any of us. There is nothing left but...but death. He is a good man, and this is...a last gesture."

He took her by the shoulders and shook her violently, feeling the mounting hurt inside him, and she said, struggling with him: "This is the country we have chosen to live in. For all of us there has been...always...the savagery moving like a dark shadow over our heads, and because we have become accustomed to it, we have looked only for laughter and we have forgotten that the savagery is always there. And now, it is wrapping itself about us. And this is the thing that Willis knows."

"He's wrong!" he said violently. "Willis is not a bloody god, he doesn't know any more than the rest of us! And I tell you we'll get out of this, one way or the other. Even that arrogant idiot Tabor knows that."

She smiled at the venom in his voice. "Tabor? He might be the man to get us out."

"The raft?" He snorted. "How the hell does he expect to get it into the water?"

She pulled away from him, held him at arms' length, and looked searchingly into his eyes. She said: "Tell me, without a lie, what you really think."

"Without a lie, I say we will be out of here in a day or two. I don't know how, but..."

"Faith? In God?"

"Call it that if you like. I just know, that's all." He pulled her close to him again and said fiercely: "I'm not just trying to comfort you, Petna, if that's what you think. I really believe it will turn out all right. Honestly. Perhaps, before, I've never really believed, deep down inside me, the things that I've said, but now... Perhaps, by believing that I was wrong, I can lose the pain of always wanting to be right. I know now that there is only one truth, that you and I will come out of this, together."

She could feel the tremor in his arms and knew that it was desire for her. There was a great sadness on her, and she wanted to say: *But I told you, Willis and I are lovers, and I can only come to you as an unclean woman,* but she could not bring herself to speak, because deep in the working of her mind there was an ancient

179

teaching, so old it had been forgotten in the drive towards the future...
It had taught her, many thousands of years ago, that a woman was a
body to be used by men, and nothing else; and now that death was so
close she could not force upon her conscious volition the abnegation
of her heritage.

She was the body of a woman, formed of flesh to be savored, of
limbs to be entwined; physical union was the fifth temptation, the
element without which worship was useless, and the search for the
void of Sunyata could only be realized through the Maha Sukha, the
ultimate embrace and the great delight. Her body was his, to be
moved by his will and not by her own, as though it were a part of him,
an extension of his own flesh and blood.

He could not know the thoughts that were racing through her
mind; he only knew that he had in his arms the woman he loved, and
that her flesh was warm and supple to his touch, and that all logic was
gone in the calenture of his need for her. He could not control his
trembling; the danger and the fear were a thousand years away, and all
that he was left with was an excitement he could not control, a heat
that seemed to burst out of him.

He looked across at the open doorway, the heavy timber door,
studded with nails in the Arab fashion, that led to the rooms
downstairs where the others were, and as if reading his thoughts, she
detached herself from him and moved across to close it silently,
leaning her slight body into it.

He said: "The way you glide when you move..."

She came back and took his hand, and moved with him into the
shadows, and he held her tight and ran his hands over her body,
feeling the softness of her waist and letting his fingers rest on the out-
curving point of the bone at her hip. He slipped a hand under her sari
and touched her breast, the nipple hard and firm, and when she tried to
pull him deeper into the shadows he unraveled the silk at her waist
and said hoarsely: "No, over where the moonlight is. I want to see
your body, every inch of it."

She lay down without a word on the hard wooden floor in the
precise center of the pale patch of moonlight, and let his hands move
over her. The floor was cold against her bare back, and she trembled
at his touch, and then there was a long shadow over her thighs in the

moonlight, and in a little while she began to moan softly and she reached up to pull him closer to her, ever closer and tighter, driving her nails into his back and clawing at him in perfect fusion.

CHAPTER 13

And now, in the darkness, the rains came.

All day long the oppressive heat had been building up, stifling them, and there had not been a cloud in the sky. But when the night came, the dark clouds raced across from the distant horizon over the mountains, heavy-laden, and suddenly the sky was torn apart with the raucous sound of the thunder. A great sheet of lightning floodlit the desert, and then the rain came down in a mighty torrent that seemed it must surely bring all the water the earth could need; but they knew that in a few hours it would be dry again, and the wasted water would have seeped away into the thirsty sand, running in rapid torrents wherever there was a *wadi*, churning up bright yellow mud that would soon dry out again and crack, leaving the soil lifeless and barren and parched once more.

The rain pounded on the tiles of the roof and poured in through the gaping holes, and under the biggest of them Willis stretched the awning from the Land Rover, tying up the corners on sticks to make a gigantic canvas bucket. He watched while the precious rain poured down on it, dirty and brown at first but then clearing as the dust was washed off the roof, and then he filled the water bottles and corked them tightly, and found empty cans and filled them, too, gathering the water together in the brightness of the lightning that flashed through the house at every monstrous clap of thunder over their heads; the old house shook with the force of the rain.

He went once to the top of the stairs and called up to M'Butu: "Are you all right up there?"

The deep voice came back to him, warring with the pounding of the rain: "I am filling my blanket with water, good water. We shall not be thirsty again."

He went back and looked at the rain for a while, watching it climb slowly up the sides of the awning, and tightened the fastenings carefully, and then went to find Tabor and handed him a full bottle with a quick smile.

He said: "You see? There are better ways to get what you want than to fight for it."

Tabor nodded, and Willis went downstairs to see if Marion was sleeping.

The candle in the big hall, shielded now in an empty can so as to give only minimum light, was far away in the corner, casting its tiny yellow glow on the sacking of the ceiling above. He whispered in the half-light: "Marion?"

The night was heavy, even with the cool of the rain, and she had taken off her trousers and shirt and was lying on top of a blanket in her underwear, half-naked and sleepless. She rolled onto one elbow to look at him.

"All the water we need...for how long?"

He handed her a bottle he had brought and she took it gratefully and drank. She sighed. "Have you got a cigarette?"

He went over to the pile of stores and rooted around until he found them, and then he sat close to her and lit one for her, looking at the red glow of the match on her long thighs. He began to envy the lovers she had had, the many lovers, and he forced himself to look away, thinking of the flowering of young bodies after his death, thinking of his Petna, upstairs now with Bradley, sleeping no doubt while her other lover watched over her. There was an emptiness inside him. He sighed and said: "You must have made many men very happy."

She drew deeply on her cigarette and said clearly: "And one man, I killed."

He knew the guilt she was feeling, and he said heavily: "I never believed that story. Even though it came from you. Even though you boasted about it." She did not answer, and he said: "I just want you to know that you never convinced me. Tabor has some theory...if the

183

facts don't seem likely...they're wrong."

"Tabor!" There was an affectionate scorn in her voice. "Tabor only wants to believe...what he wants to believe. It's true enough."

"Don't tell me, Marion, I won't listen."

She lay back on her blanket, infinitely feminine, letting the smoke from her cigarette spiral up to the ceiling, lying there in near-nakedness and completely indifferent to him, almost as though the friendship between them was closer than love, so close that she was almost part of him.

She said deliberately: "All that you know of me, Willis, even after all these years, is what you see, no more. A trollop with long legs and soft flesh who likes to get into bed with any Tom, Dick or Harry who can satisfy her. Maybe it's wrong, I don't know, I don't even care... But what I did that night...*that*, I care about now."

He knew the pain that was on her, and he waited, fearing what she would say and yet welcoming it.

She said: "Night after night my husband just sat there and got drunk, and in the course of time I learned to get drunk with him because there was nothing else I could do and maintain any sort of perspective. Have you ever been cold sober in the company of a drunk? It's intolerable, and in a while I didn't try to tolerate it, I just joined him, it was the easy way out. And you know why he got drunk? Because he wasn't good enough to join the Hunters' Association, that's why. He tried a dozen times, and each time they turned him down politely and never told him why, and each time he would come home so drunk that he could hardly stand, and one night he whipped Mohammed, the head boy, so savagely that he nearly killed him. If Mohammed had gone to the police...you know what happens to you in this country if you lay a hand on an African... But Mohammed knew the trouble I'd have if he was arrested, and so he said nothing; and he never forgave him for it, that's the kind of man he was, couldn't stand to be indebted to anyone even though he was incapable of standing on his own feet... The last time, he came in late, just back from the Association meeting, and he was so furious I was scared, not for him but for myself... He said: 'I'm a crack shot and dependable as hell, so why can't I be a white hunter, license and all, tell me that!' And, without even thinking, I said: 'You weren't very dependable the time my father needed you.' It came out without any thought behind it, and... You know, I had never consciously thought that before. I suppose that...when it happened, when Daddy was killed, I did not know what I slowly learned in the course of time, too slowly ever to realize...that when a white hunter's client gets trodden on by an elephant it's the white hunter's fault and there can be no argument about it. But it was only after I'd been out here a long time that I slowly got to know that, and it never really struck home until that night... He went white as a sheet, and I knew it was because...not because I was telling him something he didn't know, but that he knew it all along and knew that I didn't." She said bitterly: "A hundred good friends in the Colony, and no one had ever said to me: 'Your husband killed your father.' It was hard to realize that no one had ever said a word."

"Well, they wouldn't, would they?" Willis said. "Your friends didn't think much of Cassel, but you...they all loved you, for one reason or another."

She grimaced and said: "Usually for one reason."

"In spite of your...erratic behavior. No one holds it against you that you like to make love. Who doesn't?" He found himself looking at her thighs again; the temptation to stroke them was almost insupportable. He wondered if he could change her train of thought by touching her.

But she said: "From that moment on, once he knew that I knew he was responsible, how *very* responsible he had been... He said to me, very angrily: 'Who told you that, who've you been talking to?' Just as though he personally had kept it hidden from me all this time. Well, perhaps he had, I don't know anymore. He began to shout at me, to rave and fling his arms about, and he picked up that knobkerrie that hangs on the wall, and he held it out to me and shouted: 'If you ever say that again, I'll kill you, you understand? I'll kill you!' I found myself frightened of him, frightened of a drunken sot who had been responsible for the death of my own father and whom I had married... And you know why I had married him? I'll tell you, because he was...he was good in bed, that's why. If he was sober, there was no one in the world like him, but I knew that whatever love I'd had for him, whatever kind of love you like to call it, had turned that moment to pure hate. I lived with my hatred for him then, for a long time, until I just couldn't stand it anymore. He was such a good man, my father. He was quiet, and honest, and...and *good.* I knew there was only one thing I could do, and...I did it."

Willis said harshly: "I'd rather you didn't tell me."

She looked up at him and smiled then, and said: "Another of your illusions gone, but I'll tell you for a very good reason. Sure, I'm a fraud, a bloody little whore of a fraud, but I'd like at least somebody to know me for what I really am, and I'd like it to be you, Willis. I used to boast about what I'd done just to impress all those other bloody frauds, and by Christ, I did too, but with you..." She gestured hopelessly and said: "It doesn't make much sense, does it? The same truth, different reasons." She waited a little while, and then said slowly: "Yes, I killed him. I left my boyfriend in the car a little way down the road, and I walked to the house and let myself in, and there he was, drunk as a bloody coot, fast asleep on the sofa, leaning back with his legs stuck out in front of him, snoring. There was a bloody great hole in one of his socks, I remember, and I thought: *This is the man who killed my father, the man I married, a drunk with a hole in his sock...* I took hold of his hair and yanked his head back, and he didn't even stop snoring...When I let go of his hair, his head fell back onto his chest, and...I was going to shoot him, there and then, just as I'd decided on the way back with Gerald, but instead...I was drunk myself, and I blamed him for what I'd become, for making me a drunken whore... I kept thinking of the shock on my father's face if he could have seen the girl he loved so much... Slowly rotting away, physically and mentally... God, the trash his daughter had become! At that moment I was a filthy slut, a whore with her guts eaten away by alcohol... I picked up the rifle that was on the wall, and I pumped a round into it, and..." She shook her head wearily as though the haze were still there, and said: "I don't know why, I must have hit him with the poker, instead. I broke his neck like a rabbit."

She threw away the end of her cigarette, watching it smolder in the corner of the fireplace.

"As you know, there was no case for the police. They came and announced blandly that he'd been killed, and the District Officer got into the act..."

"Bradley."

"Yes, Bradley. They looked a little darkly at Gerald, but I said I'd been with him in the car all the time, so... And Mohammed told them I'd just come home and found him dead... I don't know, perhaps he was lying too, just to protect me, because he knew damn well what a phony I was and what a bastard my husband had always really been."

In the silence, she twisted her body lithely and looked at Willis and half smiled, and said: "I had to tell you. Did I spoil everything? That's the other thing I'm good at, spoiling things. But you've heard the story often enough, you could have believed it then and saved yourself some grief."

Willis said stubbornly: "I didn't believe it then, and I don't believe it now. I just don't think you're capable of murder."

"Now you're talking like Tabor. There's a great deal I'm capable of, like it or not."

Willis said carefully: "At least one of the daily papers put up a case that whoever killed him did the Colony a service. Justifiable homicide, they called it. Cassel was an evil man. He was clearly to blame in your father's death, and there were other things, too..."

"There's no such thing as justifiable homicide."

"A dozen people wanted to kill him, only they hadn't the guts. That was why...tacitly, perhaps, no one ever really tried very hard to make out a case against you."

Marion said: "The terrible thing about it all is that I was in...in a sort of coma, and still I did what I went to do. Can you imagine the kind of rottenness that makes a woman commit a murder even in a coma? How deep-rooted that rottenness must be? And all my life since then has been...consumed is the word, I suppose. It's been eating me up, the knowledge of what I did, of what I am. It even made me...so help me, it made me glad Daddy was not alive to see what I had become."

"He killed your father," Willis said steadily. "Every one of us in the Association knew that. He was dead drunk, there was absolutely no excuse for him at all."

"And I was dead drunk when I killed him. God, what a mess."

Willis groped for his words. Desperately wanting to believe it

187

himself, and not quite succeeding, he said: "I think you are punishing yourself too much, and too long. No one can measure the extent of the...the provocation. How far can you be driven before you lose control, is there anyone who can tell us that? I won't condemn you, I won't!"

"The Queen can do no wrong."

"Something like that. Till the day I die, I'll believe in you, whatever you did."

"You're talking like Tabor again."

"Am I?" He smiled. "And is that so wrong? Tabor's a good man, a man I can envy." Again he smiled and said: "For more than one reason."

"Did he ever tell you? I tried to make him love me once. He wouldn't. My first and only failure."

"No, he never said a word."

"And it was you who introduced us, you remember? God, how I wanted that man. I still do."

She ran her hands slowly down her body, and Willis looked at her and saw that she was trembling. She pulled the blanket over her body as though site were suddenly remembering modesty, and said: "He came so close to...to changing me completely."

Willis said gently: "Perhaps he still will. I know how much he feels for you."

"It's too late." She looked at him and sat up quickly and said: "Willis? I'm scared stiff of dying. Scared stiff."

There were tears in her eyes now. Willis reached out and pulled her to him, holding her tight.

He said: "We're not going to die, not yet. We'll get out of here, somehow."

He nestled his chin in the curve of her throat, and his eyes were distant and terribly sad. The rain outside was a constant, monotonous drumming, pounding at the building.

In a little while she pulled away and rubbed a hand over her face and said dryly: "They say it's good for the soul, but I'm damned if I feel any better."

"I'll get you out of here. I promise you."

"If only you could tell me *how!*"

188

"At least we have water now."

"More than my tears."

"There's the raft. It's nearly finished."

"You really think it will float?"

"If we can get it down to the water...it will float."

"And then?"

He shrugged his shoulders hopelessly: "All we have to do is to get out of range of their rifles, and that means...just a couple of hundred yards offshore."

She said again: "And then?"

"At least we'll be out of this accursed house." He looked around the great empty hall, imagining what it had once been like, when the crumbling plaster of the walls had been red with the blood of the beaten slaves. "And one day, I'll come back and blow it sky high. It's seen too much tragedy. *Darhuzuni*, you know what it means? *The Gateway To Sorrow.*"

"I know. Have you got a handkerchief?" When he gave it to her she wiped at her face and said: "And I suppose we'd better go upstairs and relieve the others."

"All right. I'll take over from M'Butu on the roof, you relieve Tabor on the south side, and we'll wake up Petna so that Bradley can get some sleep. She's...up there with him now."

Marion smiled and said lightly: "Yes, we all have our problems, don't we? Maybe I'd better wake her for you, just in case."

And, just as suddenly as it had begun, the rain stopped.

Petna awoke with a start.

She heard the faint sounds downstairs and she hastily drew her sari tighter round her waist and got to her feet.

Bradley turned away from the window and said: "It's only Willis come to wake you. Tell him I'll hang on till daylight, there's no reason why you shouldn't sleep." She shook her head and he insisted: "Tell him, my darling, I'll take your turn."

She smiled at him, touched him impulsively on the arm, and ran to the heavy timber door to swing it open. And then, she began to scream...

Mwipi, his black body gleaming in the darkness, darker than the dark itself, stood in the doorway with his *panga* raised; all she could see was the whites of his eyes. His bow and his arrows were clutched in his left hand, and he swung them at her, striking her hard on the chest and knocking her down, and as she screamed again she heard Bradley's shot and looked up to see Mwipi fling his arm forward; she heard the naked *panga* strike the wall and clatter to the floor, and then he was down on one knee and drawing his bow, moving with incredible, silent speed, loosing off two arrows in the darkness and then racing forward past her. She heard no sound from Bradley, and then Willis came racing up the stairs and she heard three more shots in rapid succession, heard Willis call out savagely: "A light! Marion, the flashlight!"

Petna ran back towards Bradley and stumbled over a recumbent form, and when she groped at it fearfully, there was the slime of blood on her hands, and she clutched the body to her and dropped it with horror when she saw that it was black...

Now the room was suddenly alive, and the bright beam of the flashlight showed her the body of the African on the floor, his face shot away, and then it swung over to find Bradley...

She stared at him in horror. He hung from the window, transfixed to the heavy mullion by the birchwood shaft that had gone through his chest. His feet slumped on the floor, and as she watched, the arrowhead came away and he fell over sideways to the floor and lay still, and she ran to him hysterically and pulled the long arrow from his body, knowing that if she could take away the instrument of death, death itself would go; but he was quite lifeless, his eyes wide open in an expression of shocked surprise. She held him tightly and began to rock from side to side, moaning.

Willis called out angrily: "They're in the house, for God's sake get some more light..." He was like a madman, running first to the veranda and then back to the door, yelling: Tabor! Come quickly! They're all around us!"

He heard Tabor's answering call, loud and yet calm: "Up onto the roof, everybody!"

He grabbed at Petna and pulled her angrily away, and she wailed and tried to remain, but he carried her by brute force with him, and thrust her towards Marion and said: Up onto the roof, quick, both of you!"

Marion did not hesitate. She pulled at Petna and dragged her up the stairway, and then M'Butu was suddenly there beside them, his huge bulk towering over them on the upper step. The rifle was still slung across his back, but his right hand clutched his long knife and it was red with blood.

He said thickly: "One more on the roof, a dead man now... Search the house while I take care of the women." He pushed at Marion and said: "In there, the small room, both of you..."

It was a tiny closet at the top of the stairs, thick-walled and windowless, and Marion answered him angrily: "The hell with that, look after Petna..."

M'Butu nodded. He took Petna's arm and said gently: "In here, Memsahib, in here..." He guided her into the little room and stood by the door, his knife ready, waiting, watching in the darkness, his eyes narrowed and savage.

They all stood on the stairway, waiting, listening, and Willis said, whispering: "God knows how many more of them got in... I'll take the flashlight. Cover me on both sides, Tabor."

Room by room, they began to move through the old house, and the only sound they heard was the faint wailing that came from the room at the top of the stairs. The beam of the light played over the crumbling walls, the fallen timbers, the rotting doors, and when, at last, they had finished they went back to the stairs where M'Butu was waiting for them.

Willis said wearily: "Nothing. Only two of them? I don't believe it."

"Maybe," M'Butu said. "Maybe. Many men would make more noise. They knew they had to be quiet. *Bwana* Bradley?"

Willis' voice was heavy: "Dead."

M'Butu looked at him and said nothing.

Tabor swung the beam of the light down the stairway and asked: "Were we wrong to hold the whole house? Maybe if we'd tried to keep one room only...?"

"They would have burned us out," M'Butu said. "No, we must still hold all of it. If they take as much as one room...if they bring their

191

firebrands close enough..." He raised a huge hand didactically and said: "We must keep them all out in the open, all of them. And now we must wait for them to come again. If they learn they have succeeded only to this extent...they will come again."

"How the bloody hell did they get in?" Exasperated beyond the limits of patience, Willis swore softly. "The ground floor windows were all within sight of...of somebody. Up the front of the house on the outside?"

Tabor shook his head. "Ever since I saw Petna come down there when Baba was killed...I was watching it. The columns over the portico, could they climb those?"

Willis blinked the weariness away, and his voice was hollow. "As soon as it's light, that's a thing we'll have to find out. There's a way into the house somewhere and we've got to find it."

A heavy, melancholic silence fell over them. In the darkness, M'Butu was staring ahead of him, his eyes unemotional, stolid, composed. He looked back at Petna with great compassion, listening to the muted sound of her wailing, and he looked at the anger and the fear in Marion's eyes, and then he touched the broken elbow where the Somali stone had struck. He said to himself: *What I have to do, I should have done before. Before this happened.*

And then a great feeling of ease slowly settled over him. He thought: It is only a chance, a very small chance. My father used to tell me: 'You are not worthy of my blood if you will not give everything you have for your tribe, your family, and your friends.'

He thought for a while of his childhood days, of his life as a young man, and of the days of splendor when he was a chief; it worried him that the height of his power had been so long ago, that so many years had passed in the gentle decline into impotence that had left him, as he was now, as no more than other men. He thrust the evil of the thought away from him, and he knew that the qualities that made a chief great were still there, inside him, ready to be used when the need arose; it gave him great comfort.

CHAPTER 14

The red striation in the east began to turn to yellow; and then the sun burst out of the sky and covered the land.

In the house of Darhuzuni, there was the smell of death again, a sour stench that had dried out in the long years since the slavers had left there, and which had now returned as though to show them that this was the scent of Africa itself.

Since the death of Bradley, Petna had hardly spoken a word. She had taken a canvas bag from the stores, had filled it with cartridges for the shotgun, and had slung it around her waist on a piece of string, and she stood now at the northern window on the upper floor, no longer hiding herself in fear, but standing straight and resolute and icy cold.

Beside her, worrying, Marion said: "Will you be all right? We just can't hold the house anymore, not for another night, there just aren't enough of us. If they get in again...Tabor and I want to go down to the cellars, to see if we can force a way out and down to the beach. I don't know how, but..." Her voice trailed away, her thought unfinished.

Petna nodded, not looking at her. She said: "I am not afraid, Marion, not anymore. Go and search."

Wearily, Marion went off to find Tabor. She found him with Willis, and said hesitantly: "I wonder... Should I do this by myself? Or you? If they come again..."

Tabor said shortly: "No. I want you with me." She looked at him in surprise, and when she turned to Willis he looked away from

193

ALAN CAILLOU

her, knowing that the hope was going there, too, and not wanting to comment on it. He said gently: "They won't come yet, not after last night. But don't be too long."

The raft was finished, as finished as it ever would be, and when they went downstairs they looked at it for a while, wondering about it. It was a reflection of their frustration, crude, ungainly, and showed little promise of help to them; a dozen timbers had been hammered together with bolts and nails and pegs—with anything that would serve to join one spar to another, and the empty gasoline cans had been strapped underneath it, and a long beam had been hacked into the semblance of an oar with a *machete* and was lashed to a single rowlock in the stern with a leather strap.

Marion looked at it with despair and said: "It will never float, never, and we'll never get it to the beach anyway."

Tabor shook his head. He turned to her and held her shoulders and said gravely: "The scope of human tenacity... You never know until you try, and then, sometimes you can work wonders. We'll get it down there, somehow, and it will float." There was a tiredness in his voice, but he smiled at her and said: "It will take us out of here because it must, there's no other way, no other hope for us. So let's go find those cellars."

When he turned away he took her hand, quite naturally, and they went together down to the broken stairway that led to the ancient cisterns. With a timber left over from the raft they shouldered aside the rubble that lay in their way and forced a passage to the gaping hole in the floor that marked the place where once stairs had been, stone steps that now lay in a worthless pile far below them. They fetched the rope and a flashlight, and Tabor lit a piece of paper and threw it down and watched it burn brightly twelve feet below them and he said:

"The smoke is moving, there's air coming in there somewhere."

"Of course. It leads to the old cave, the slave pit. But that's a long way up from the beach."

"Our rope might reach it."

"The rope is a hundred feet long. The cave is twice that much above the water."

She felt him squeeze her hand. "We don't know it's impossible

194

till we try it, do we?"

"No. No, I suppose not."

"Then come on."

He lowered her down into the darkness, threw down the flashlight, and then he tied the rope to the heavy mullion of the window and slid down after her. They groped around for a moment, feeling for the passage of air, stumbling on the uneven surface of the tunnel they were in, and then set off slowly in the humid darkness.

The tunnel smelt of bats. They fluttered out in their hundreds, in thousands, as they groped their way along. They began with a sudden rustling sound as they were disturbed in their age-old cavities, and they began to beat against the walls in their terror, wheeling and descending about them so that Marion crouched low and covered her hair with her hands, grimacing.

Tabor put his arm around her quickly and said: "It's all right, it means there's a way out."

When she looked at him he was smiling and he said: "Don't tell me you're scared of bats?"

They waited till the noise and the rush had gone and only the stink of them hung in the air, nauseating them, as strong as strong ammonia, and then they carefully crawled over the boulders and the jagged rocks that lined the floor, standing up sometimes when the rock ceiling was high above them, and sometimes lying down and dragging themselves laboriously along, down and down, down so steeply that sometimes they wondered if they would ever be able to climb back up again.

Soon they came to the beginnings of the great cave itself, and there were iron rings set in the walls, and pieces of heavy chain hung from them.

The cave broadened out, and soon the fresh air came to them in great welcome gusts, and when they reached the light that was the broad expanse of the day outside it was blinding in its blue intensity. The opening in the cliff-face was more than eighty feet across, and the probing fingers of roots hung down from its ceiling, and the escarpment dropped away at their feet steeply down to the sea, a precipitous course of broken rock and jagged stone, and as they watched a seagull dropped away from the edge and wheeled sharply out to sea.

Tabor said, and there was triumph in his voice: "There must have been steps down there once... If we can find them, reach them with the rope. "

The water broke against the reef a hundred and fifty feet below them, and the cliff was sheer, steep, forbidding any descent. Tabor was staring down, looking for a ledge, and Marion sank down to the ground behind him, not looking out with him.

He turned back to her in surprise and she said wearily: "I know. Willis told me. There is no way down, no way at all. The steps were all chiseled away, years and years ago, there's no way down."

"You knew? And yet you came..."

"To get away from the smell of death. To get away from   that awful house."

"If we could throw the raft down there..."

She said impatiently: "For God's sake, it won't survive the impact. And if it does...we'd have more than fifty feet to drop from the end of the rope, onto the rocks. I tell you it's hopeless."

He had never seen her so anguished. He came and crouched down beside her and said urgently: "But we must *try!* We'll drag the raft down here and throw it over the edge, and then..."

When he paused, she looked at him expectantly, as though the impossible could be done because he said it could. He raised his hands and clutched at an image and said: "I *won't* believe it can't be done!"

Suddenly, she began to cry softly, and he put his arms around her and said: "Nothing is as bad as it seems, we're still alive, there's still hope for all of us..."

"Hope!"

"Everything man ever accomplished was done through hope."

"Stop preaching at me, for Christ's sake, and give me a handkerchief."

Instead, he put out his hand and gently wiped the tears from her face with the tips of his fingers. "A little while ago I would not have believed you were capable of tears. Is the wall coming down?"

"The wall?"

He smiled. "Willis said...we were...gossiping about you. He said you'd built a wall around yourself and he wanted to see it breached and find the true Marion behind it. I guess I wanted that too. I've wanted it for a long time. Ever since..." Her eyes were holding his. He said gravely: You remember that day by the lake? You lost your camera and I promised you a new one."

"I lost a good deal more, didn't I?"

He did not answer her. Instead, he stood up and went to the edge of the cave and looked out across the sea, the onshore breeze catching his hair and ruffling it.

He said: "It looks so fresh and clean out there, a thousand miles of everything that is good, and yet, up there above us there's all the filth in the world."

She was surprised at the sudden vehemence in his voice. He said, almost angrily: "I came to Africa to hunt, and I stayed to love, and maybe I stayed too long because the love is beginning to turn to hate, and that's a thing I can't forgive them for."

He turned to look at her, standing apart, and said: "You remember? I told you, that day, that I was getting a surfeit of the killing. When Willis came to me about this safari of ours he said there'd be no shooting, and once, not so long ago, it was only the hunting I was interested in. But I'd gotten tired of the killing, and..." He sighed. "Now, it's men we're killing. Is that part of the story? Are they just animals?"

"We're defending ourselves, that's all it is."

"Yes, I know that."

"But shooting or not, you came." There was a need for her to urge him to continue.

He smiled and said: "Yes, I came. Not so long ago I'd have told him, hell, if I can't shoot anything, if I can't get myself a trophy to prove what a hell of a man I am... But instead I said yes, I'll join you. Maybe it was because I knew you were coming along too, because maybe at last I'd have a better chance to...to get to know you better. The last time we really said anything to each other...it wasn't a great success, was it?"

She shivered at the memory, and said: "Down here, with the sea and the fresh air so close, it's easy to forget that up there... The danger isn't very far away, we should get back."

"I know." He did not move. "I remember you covered from head to foot with black mud and still contriving to look...feminine. An animal out of the slime, draped in primeval mud, but a gloriously feminine animal. I wanted you so badly that day, but...to myself alone."

"Two years ago. A lot has happened since then."

"A lot has happened in the last few days." He moved towards her slowly, and she began to tremble, knowing, waiting. He put down his hands and raised her to her feet and pulled her tight to him and said: "Do you trust me, Marion? Do you trust me to get you out of here, one way or another, without asking how because I don't know how?"

"Yes. I trust you." There was a new freedom on her, because even if the danger was still there, not far away in time or in distance, there was...she said aloud, "Someone to lean on." It had never, before, seemed so important to her. She felt herself clutching at him, and she said fiercely: "Yes, I trust you."

He held her face in his hands and kissed her, and when she held him tightly he disengaged himself and said: "When the battle is over... One way or another it will be over soon. I love you, Marion. I want you to be my wife."

She put her arms around him and reached up to kiss him, gently, holding back the yearning that was in her, letting only the tenderness go to him, letting him take from her only what he wanted and negating the rest because she knew that now it was only a matter of time. His arms were strong about her, strong and rigid and possessive. And when he released her, there was almost a mockery in his voice. He said: "And now let's go back and tell the others there's no way out."

When she looked at him and sighed, he took her hand and led her back towards the tunnel that led to the cellars of the house.

All the fear had gone, and it was as though the danger had quite receded. Slowly, holding hands once more like lovers, they began the long ascent to the menace and the fear and the sorrow that were up there within the old stone walls.

* * *

198

All night long the Captain had waited in the gulley.

The men who were with him were silent, disturbed, afraid. The sound of the shooting had told them the story, and they looked at the Captain, knowing the deep love he had for his son, and said nothing to him. Some of them were whispering among themselves, knowing that there was a serious rift in their ranks over the matter of the witch doctor and the *maji-maji* bullets that would turn to water but did not, but instead had killed Owadi, who was very popular among them. They thought it must be because of the argument the witch doctor had had with the Captain, the argument which, in the end, had told them all what was going to happen...

It would all be so simple, they thought, if only their leader (who, after all, was a foreigner from another tribe) would listen to the wise words of the old and evil *mchawi*; but instead, he had chosen to taunt the old man, and the witch doctor had said, eyeing him with so much venom that some of them trembled: "Fight this fight the way you will; but if you do not listen to my words, then I see only evil and the swift approach of death."

"Whose death, old man?" the Captain had asked, mocking. And the *mchawi*, not wanting to commit himself or to make himself look ridiculous in front of the men from his own tribe, had answered, mumbling: "The death of one who is greatly loved." He had turned away in a sulk and gone back to the village with his bodyguard, to sit in front of his hut and worry about ways to punish the Captain for his arrogance.

And now, they were sure, he would want them to rush the fortress, and they were frightened to do this, because now there was not even the old witch doctor to turn the *pepo*, the spirit of evil, away from them and towards the white men; they wanted so badly to go back to their homes, but they were frightened, too, of the anger of the Captain.

And so they drew apart, and whispered, and waited, throwing him surreptitious glances as he sat there in the sand, cross-legged, his rifle unattended at his side, his head thrown back against the dry sandstone, his eyes immobile. One of the men was watching a bluefly that was crawling over the Captain's wounded cheek, and when it crawled over the eyeball the Captain did not blink, nor did he move when it began to feed on the clotted blood of the gray bandage; he was as motionless as death itself.

One of the men, who was known as Mhuni, the Shiftless One, crawled over to the edge of the gulley and cautiously raised his head to look at the house; he was startled to find that in the daylight it was so terribly close, and he looked back fearfully to the cluster of rocks where the others were, knowing that he should have stayed there with them and not come with the Captain on this suicidal mission.

He stared at the house, and as he watched he saw a movement on the roof, and M'Butu was there, Juma M'Butu the Chief from Mwadi whom the terrible old *mchawi* had wanted to kill because of a long-past insult, and he was clutching a limp body in his huge arms and striding to the edge of the overhang and looking out, far out to where the rocks were. One of his arms was heavily wrapped in bandages, and he moved with painful slowness.

Mhuni said swiftly: "Captain! M'Butu! And your son! Quickly!"

Now, a sudden and angry energy took possession of the Captain. He reached for his rifle and wormed his way across the gully and went to Mhuni and looked at the house, and he saw M'Butu bend down and put the body of Mwipi on the roof at his feet and then stand up and throw out his arms to the sky, and he heard the passionate voice, deep and steady but full of sadness, calling out across the scrub, calling loudly, sending the powerful resonance of it rolling across the desert to the rocks:

"*Watu!* People! Listen to me!"

He stood there like a giant Messiah, his arms flung out, the broken elbow lending a stark angularity, the fingers spread as though groping to the skies for coherence, a big, solid man of tremendous dignity, his long robe falling to his feet, his body solid and strong.

The Captain raised his head in bewilderment and watched.

M'Butu called again: "*Watu!* Come from your hiding place and listen to me!"

The Captain turned his head and looked back. From the rocks, from the shadows of the great boulders, some of his men were slowly creeping, crouching together in the shadows and watching. He looked again at M'Butu, fascinated, and as he watched he heard M'Butu call

200

out, angry with pain and heaviness:

"Listen to me, fools! You cannot take this house because it is too strong for you, and many more of you will die if you do not leave these strong defenders in peace! Is it my life you want? Then I will give it to you, I give myself to you! I will come down among you and you may kill me, you may drink my blood and I pray that my wisdom will pass to you as my strength does, but let my friends go in peace! I command you! Let them go in peace! Once, I was your chief, and as I now die I tell you, I will always be your chief and this is my last command: Let the white men go!"

At the rocks, the men were huddling in uneasy groups, listening, watching, wondering about the Captain, wondering why he did not use his rifle. One of them looked at the sand between the rocks and the house, counting the dead who lay there, knowing that the hyenas had taken many of them away. Listening to the strong voice, reaching out more easily than their ill-aimed bullets could reach, they shuddered, wanting to hide from the virulent anger and finding no comfort in the nearness of their fellows because their fellows were cheerless too. And so, they watched and waited.

M'Butu bent down and raised the limp body that was at his feet, raised it high above his head on his outstretched hands, and they watched, fearfully.

In the gulley, the Captain stared, hypnotized by the sight of his son, and all that the witch doctor had said came back to him, and there was a terrible anguish inside him, and he raised himself up to his full height, standing on stocky legs and staring at M'Butu, no longer hiding himself but standing in the open with all the fear gone, staring at the useless body that had been his son, that once had been called Mwipi the Brave One.

M'Butu raised his voice again and shouted: "This is a man who came into the house and he is dead! I give him to you that you may learn!"

For a moment, the body was poised there, high in the air against the pale morning sky, limp and soft and spineless and wasted, and M'Butu groaned at the pain that was rushing through his arm, groaned once, and then hurled the body forward and down to the ground.

The Captain watched, frozen in shock, and Mhuni pulled back

201

his bowstring and loosed off a quick arrow, hardly stopping to aim, firing instinctively as he had been taught from his earliest youth; he saw the short arrow bury itself in M'Butu's chest, saw the look of shocked surprise as the Chief swung around to face the flank attack, saw him clutch at the shaft with his left hand and pull it out...

He heard him still calling, his voice only momentarily interrupted: "Then kill me if you must, but let my friends go free!"

Over by the rocks there was only silence, for the men gathered there were leaderless and there was no one to tell them what to do, and so they stood close by their cover and they watched, in silence and in a heavy fear; but in the gulley, where the Captain stood rooted to the ground, his feet wide-spaced and solid, with the weight of his heart pulling him back into the sand he had sprung from, Mhuni shot another arrow and another, and then three more until his quiver was empty, and for a little while he, too, stared at M'Butu, saw him standing firm and strong with his arm now limply hanging to his side as though the effort he had exerted had been the last flush of activity; there were four arrows piercing his body, and the last had struck him in the side of the neck.

And then Mhuni took his spear, the seven-foot Masai spear he carried because of the prestige it gave him, and hurled it high into the air, drawing back his arm and swinging his shoulder forward with its flight. It went smoothly, silently upward in a graceful arc, then gathered speed as the descent began, and entered M'Butu's stomach, and he twisted around with the force of it, and staggered for a moment, and then fell crashing to the ground far below and did not move or make any sound again.

And then, the Captain screamed and raced across the sand to his son, and took the limp head in his arms, and cradled the useless, inanimate body, and swayed from side to side, moaning: "My son, my son...my son..." as though all that he had ever lived for, had ever believed in, had been suddenly, cruelly negated. His black, scarred face, with the bloodied bandage still seeping, was streaked with his tears.

On the roof, high above him, scrambling in stupefaction to the edge of the portico, Willis raised his rifle. His face was taut, savage, grim. And then Tabor was suddenly beside him, panting hard from the run across the broken tiles of Darhuzuni's roof, and he was gripping the barrel of the rifle and saying urgently: "No, Willis, don't shoot. Leave him."

Willis turned and stared, and there was a dark anger in his eyes, but Tabor said again, insisting quietly: "Don't shoot."

He could see the fury bursting out, the bitter fury of desperation, controlled because of the deep friendship but explosive none the less because the chance had come to cut off the head and so destroy, perhaps, the arms. Willis said with savage impatience: "You bloody fool, that's their leader, look at his uniform!"

When Tabor held onto the rifle and shook his head, he shouted: "Have you lost your bloody reason? It's their leader, I tell you!"

He swore furiously, angry with himself for the quarrel, angry with Tabor for the sudden certainty of authority, and Tabor said, meeting his anger: "There are better ways to get what you want than to fight for it. Your own words, Willis. And M'Butu had the answer, if I'd only listened... The time for reason has come."

"M'Butu! We were too slow to save him, but at least we can hit them for him..."

"No."

"For God's sake! They've hit us hard and we have to hit back, harder!"

"The answer to savagery is not more savagery."

"No? Then what the hell is it?"

"Now is the time to find out."

The anger had gone, and an intense despair had taken its place. Tabor said again, making an order of it: "Hold your fire."

There was a moment of tension, almost a struggle with the rifle, and then Tabor released his grip on the barrel and Willis lowered it to his side and waited.

Tabor said again, his voice low and urgent: "You understand? Don't fire."

And then he turned away and Willis looked after him, and hurried across the roof and back to the stairway.

All that the Captain could think of was the great gulf that had split his family wide open, had torn the love brutally out of his heart to mock him with its uselessness.

He looked at the broken body of M'Butu and at the limp form of his own dead son, and he said to himself: "There lies a man who was once a great chief, and here is a young man who would one day have become a great leader, and they are both dead."

He clutched tighter at his son, trying to bring back the life to the dead flesh, trying to wash the guilt away with the tears, trying to bring back the fine life of the past when the crops had been good and the sun had been hot on their backs as they hunted together, the short stocky man with the muscular legs and the tall slim youth in whom all his love had rested.

Anil when he looked up, Tabor was close beside him, and he was unarmed.

The Captain did not speak because there were no words he could use, and Tabor slowly held his arms out from his sides, explaining something, and when the Captain said, dully: "Why do you not kill me now?"

Tabor said gently: "I come to you with no weapons."

The Captain laid the body of his son on the earth, and stood up, looking at Tabor unafraid because even death could not frighten him now.

He said slowly, not understanding: "It is with your hands you want to kill me? What kind of man are you? You are worse than *they* are, a man who would twist the pain of a father while you choke the life out of him."

And Tabor said: "I have not come to kill you. I have come to tell you to go to your home, to go back to your village, to your family."

The Captain's eyes dropped briefly. "My family is here, all that is left of it."

"Your son?"

"My son."

"You have other sons?"

"No other sons."

"I am sorry. I too know what it is to lose someone you love."

The Captain looked again at the motionless body and said: "He was nothing to you. Why should you be sorry?"

"If we can feel the pain that other people feel, perhaps we will all be better men. I feel for your son, and I ask you to feel for those we have lost."

The Captain could not fight the tears that humbled him. He said brokenly: "I loved my son."

"And this is the price you pay...for what?"

For a long time, the Captain did not answer. He was trying to drive back the tears, conscious above everything of his uniform, conscious of the three stars his wife had sewn into his cap to show that he was an officer and a leader of other men.

He said quietly: "I do not know for what."

He could feel that above him, at the window of the second floor of the old house, there were white faces watching him. He looked up, praying that a rifle would be fired and put an end to him, but all he saw were the faces of the hunter, and the woman he had promised to his son, and the dark, somber face of the young Asian girl. There were no guns to be seen, and the three of them were watching him, gravely; he fancied that there was compassion in the eyes of the white girl, and suddenly all the hatred seemed a foolish thing for children to play with, but now it was too late to learn this.

He looked back at Tabor and begged: "Kill me now, *Bwana*. Kill me."

The *Bwana* was a natural honorific, as though there could be no other form of address at all. He said again: "Kill me, *Bwana*, and without me my men will run from you and you, too, can go back to your family."

"No. I will not kill you. Take your son and bury him, and we will bury our dead, and then you must lead your men away from here."

The heat of the day was building up as they stood there, the hot sun striking fiercely, impatiently at them, as though the cold of the night had never been anything more than a dream to be forgotten until the dark should come again to remind them of it.

As far as they could see, the great empty desert was broken only by the patches of dried-out thorn and the stark shadows of the rocks, as though beyond the confines of Darhuzuni and its dried-up well there was nothing but oblivion; it seemed that nothing could live out there in the wasted soil that the long hot centuries had burned till only arid sand remained.

Tabor said: "Take your men away from here. Take them back to their villages and let them count the deaths they have suffered. And we too will go home."

For a long time the Captain stared at him, and then he looked up once at the weary faces above him, and then he bent down slowly and picked up the body of his son. He cradled it in his thick arms and turned away and walked slowly out into the desert.

Tabor watched him go, and when he was a long way away, he turned on his heel and went back into the house.

It was midday by the heat of the sun when the cloud of dust that was the *watu* began to move away from the shadows of the rocks, moving north in ragged, ungainly columns, moving in small, scattered groups with no feeling of victory or defeat, not knowing where they were really going, but knowing only that the battle, for the moment, was over; the rest would take care of itself.

For almost two hours Marion had watched them, standing on the roof above the portico and using the binoculars, holding the receding dust cloud in the lens and letting the flood of relief drive away the apprehension that still nagged at her mind.

Petna, silent and morose, stood beside her, waiting, watching the compound where Tailor and Willis worked with their shovels. When she began to cry softly, Marion put an arm over her shoulder, feeling how frail a thing a crying woman could be, and said: "It's all over now, Petna. It's all over."

Petna shivered and would not speak. Marion said: "They are making the graves close to the well so that they will be together."

The wide, lost eyes stared back at her, not understanding, and the voice was a whisper. "My father, and my lover, both at once..." The veil cleared from her eyes, and she said: "In all the time we were together, Bradley and I, he never once touched me until last night, in all those years... Last night he left his seed in my body and then he died, and now... Now there is nothing. I hoped with him to find

Sunyata, and I did not find it... Instead, it came to the man who loved me. Is this what Sunyata really means? The Great Void?"

She brushed a hand across her face and said again: "My father, and the man who loved me. *Sunyata.*" She turned away, and when Marion moved to go with her she put out a hand and said gently: "No, let me go to them alone." She moved slowly across the rooftop and down the stairs.

For Marion, it was as though all the energy had gone from her and left a vacuum behind it, a vacuum in which even the thoughts would not come; it was as though the whole course of her life had been building up to a moment of supreme elation, and that now the moment was here and was nothing more than an anamorphosis.

She sank down to her knees and let her body go back onto the hot tiles, and she lay for a long time and looked up at the sky, her arms outflung as though she herself were a sacrifice, letting the heavy load of responsibility go from her but feeling unsubstantial without it. She wanted to sleep.

And when Tabor and Willis came to look for her, she said: "She's a lost child, you'll have to take care of her, Willis."

Willis wiped at the sweat and the sand on his face. "Yes, I know that." He looked around him and said: "Where is she?"

"She went to the graves."

Tabor said sharply: "No, she didn't..." For a moment, Willis stared at him, and then Tabor was running fast, across the roof, slipping on the loose tiles and stumbling towards the head of the stairs, calling out: "Petna! Petna!" And then he was gone.

They found her, the three of them together, in the small room where M'Butu had stood guard over her. She was curled up on the floor, her knees drawn up to her breast, and the stones were red and shining with the blood that had come from her wrists.

Willis, as silent as she was, crouched over her and touched her shoulder, and they saw him shudder. When they turned away he looked up and said: "Go on ahead, move south along the coast. Take the water and the rifles."

Marion hesitated, and there was sudden alarm on her white face, but Tabor took her by the arm and led her gently away, and they went downstairs and into the great hall where the futile raft was propped up against the decaying wall, never to be used, and out into the bright sunlight where the graves were; and they waited a while and then gathered up the rifles and the water bottles, and clambered over the broken wall and went out into the hostile desert.

When Marion paused to look back at the house, Tabor turned and said: "Are you coming?"

They walked together slowly and in silence for an hour, and then they sat down to rest in the shade of a giant umbrella-thorn, and stared out across the sea and waited, forcing their thoughts to the long trek home across the wide white sands that were soaking up the sun, parched again after the night's rain and showing no sign, as they never would show signs, of all the blood that had run there.

It was silent, and lonely, and vast, and empty; and when at last the small figure of Willis came towards them, the house of Darhuzuni was only a pile of stones behind him, a cipher in the distance; it was an alien and crumbling necropolis, and the only sounds made there were the whispering voices of the dead.

THE END

ABOUT THE AUTHOR

Alan Lyle-Smythe was born in Surrey, England. Prior to World War II, he served with the Palestine Police from 1936 to 1939 and learned the Arabic language. He was awarded an MBE in June 1938. He married Aliza Sverdova in 1939, then studied acting from 1939 to 1941.

In January 1940, Lyle-Smythe was commissioned in the Royal Army Service Corps. Due to his linguistic skills, he transferred to the Intelligence Corps and served in the Western Desert, in which he used the surname "Caillou" (the French word for 'pebble') as an alias.

He was captured in North Africa, imprisoned and threatened with execution in Italy, then escaped to join the British forces at Salerno. He was then posted to serve with the partisans in Yugoslavia. He wrote about his experiences in the book The World is Six Feet Square (1954). He was promoted to captain and awarded the Military Cross in 1944.

Following the war, he returned to the Palestine Police from 1946 to 1947, then served as a Police Commissioner in British-occupied Italian Somaliland from 1947 to 1952, where he was recommissioned a captain.

After work as a District Officer in Somalia and professional hunter, Lyle-Smythe travelled to Canada, where he worked as a hunter and then became an actor on Canadian television.

He wrote his first novel, Rogue's Gambit, in 1955, first using the name Caillou, one of his aliases from the war. Moving from Vancouver to Hollywood, he made an appearance as a contestant on the January 23 1958 edition of You Bet Your Life.

He appeared as an actor and/or worked as a screenwriter in such shows as Daktari, The Man From U.N.C.L.E. (including the screenwriting for "The Bow-Wow Affair" from 1965), Thriller, Daniel Boone, Quark, Centennial, and How the West Was Won. In 1966-67, he had a recurring role (as Jason Flood) in NBC's "Tarzan" TV series starring Ron Ely. Caillou appeared in such television movies as Sole Survivor (1970), The Hound of the Baskervilles (1972, as Inspector Lestrade), and Goliath Awaits (1981). His cinema film credits included roles in Five Weeks in a Balloon (1962), Clarence, the Cross-Eyed Lion (1965), The Rare Breed (1966), The Devil's Brigade (1968), Hellfighters (1968), Everything You Always Wanted to Know About Sex* (*But Were Afraid to Ask) (1972), Herbie Goes to Monte Carlo (1977), Beyond Evil (1980), The Sword and the Sorcerer (1982) and The Ice Pirates (1984).

Caillou wrote 52 paperback thrillers under his own name and the nom de plume of Alex Webb, with such heroes as Cabot Cain, Colonel Matthew Tobin, Mike Benasque, Ian Quayle and Josh Dekker, as well as writing many magazine stories.

Several of Caillou's novels were made into films, such as Rampage with Robert Mitchum in 1963, based on his big game hunting knowledge; Assault on Agathon, for which Caillou did the screenplay as well; and The Cheetahs, filmed in 1989.

He was married to Aliza Sverdova from 1939 until his death. Their daughter Nadia Caillou was the screenwriter for the film Skeleton Coast.

Alan Caillou died in Sedona, Arizona in 2006.

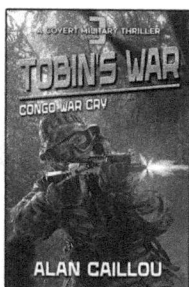

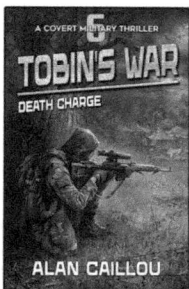

ADDITIONAL ACTION & ADVENTURE
FROM ALAN CAILLOU

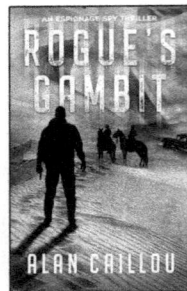

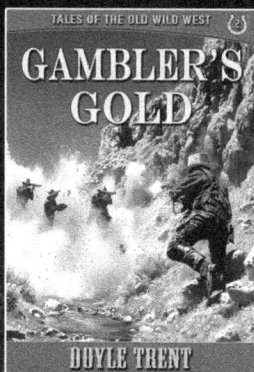

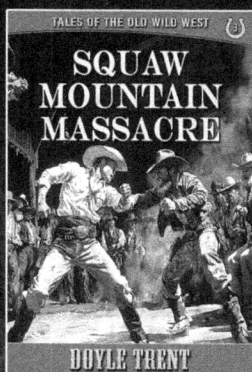

DON'T MISS ANY OF MICHAEL KASNER'S HARD HITTING MILITARY NOVEL SERIES

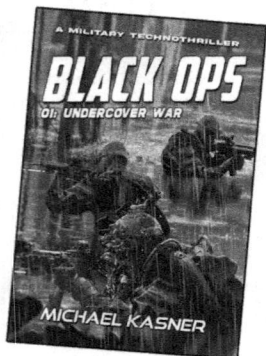

BLACK OPS

Formed by an elite cadre of government officials, the Black OPS team goes where the law can't - to seek retribution for acts of terror directed against Americans anywhere in the world.

3 BOOK SERIES

WARKEEP 2030

Armed with all the tactical advantages of modern technology, battle hard and ready when the free world is threatened - the Peacekeepers are the baddest grunts on the planet.

4 BOOK SERIES

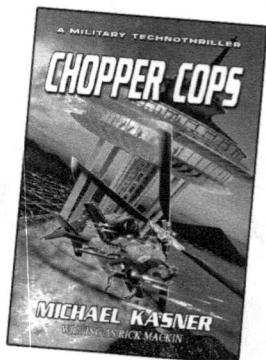

CHOPPER COPS

America is being torn apart as criminal cartels terrorize our cities, dealing drugs and death wholesale. Local police are outgunned, so the President unleashes the U.S. TACTICAL POLICE FORCE. An elite army of super cops with ammo to burn, they swoop down on the hot spots in sleek high-tech attack choppers to win the dirty war and take back America!

4 BOOK SERIES

FROM CALIBER BOOKS
www.calibercomics.com

CALIBER
BOOKS

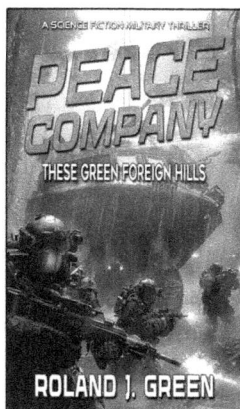

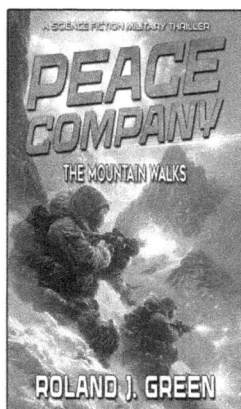

DON'T MISS ANY OF NEIL HUNTER'S NOVELS FROM CALIBER BOOKS

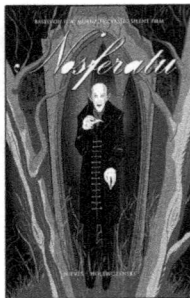

ALSO AVAILABLE FROM CALIBER COMICS

QUALITY GRAPHIC NOVELS TO ENTERTAIN

THE SEARCHERS: VOLUME 1
The Shape of Things to Come

Before *League of Extraordinary Gentlemen* there was *The Searchers*. At the dawn of the 20th Century the greatest literary adventurers from the minds of Wells, Doyle, Burroughs, and Haggard were created. All thought to be the work of pure fiction. However, a century later, the real-life descendents of those famous characters are recuited by the legendary Professor Challenger in order to save mankind's future. Series collected for the first time.

"Searchers is the comic book I have on the wall with a sign reading - 'Love books? Never read a comic? Try this one! ...money back guarantee...'" - Dark Star Books.

WAR OF THE WORLDS: INFESTATION

Based on the H.G. Wells classic! The "Martian Invasion" has begun again and now mankind must fight for its very humanity. It happened slowly at first but by the third year, it seemed that the war was almost over... the war was almost lost.

"Writer Randy Zimmerman has a fine grasp of drama, and spins the various strands of the story into a coherent whole... imaginative and very gritty."
- war-of-the-worlds.co.uk

HELSING: LEGACY BORN

From writer Gary Reed (Deadworld) and artists John Lowe (Captain America), Bruce McCorkindale (Godzilla). She was born into a legacy she wanted no part of and pushed into a battle recessed deep in the shadows of the night. Samantha Helsing is torn between two worlds...two allegiances...two families. The legacy of the Van Helsing family and their crusade against the "night creatures" comes to modern day with the most unlikely of all warriors.

"Congratulations on this masterpiece..."
- Paul Dale Roberts, Compuserve Reviews

DEADWORLD

Before there was The Walking Dead there was Deadworld. Here is an introduction of the long running classic horror series, Deadworld, to a new audience! Considered by many to be the godfather of the original zombie comic with over 100 issues and graphic novels in print and over 1,000,000 copies sold, Deadworld ripped into the undead with intelligent zombies on a mission and a group of poor teens riding in a school bus desperately try to stay one step ahead of the sadistic, Harley-riding King Zombie. Death, mayhem, and a touch of supernatural evil made Deadworld a classic and now here's your chance to get into the story!

DAYS OF WRATH

Award winning comic writer & artist Wayne Vansant brings his gripping World War II saga of war in the Pacific to Guadalcanal and the Battle of Bloody Ridge. This is the powerful story of the long, vicious battle for Guadalcanal that occurred in 1942-43. When the U.S. Navy orders its outnumbered and out-gunned ships to run from the Japanese fleet, they abandon American troops on a bloody, battered island in the South Pacific.

"Heavy on authenticity, compellingly written and beautifully drawn."
- Comics Buyers Guide

SHERLOCK HOLMES:
THE CASE OF THE MISSING MARTIAN

Sherlock is called out of retirement to London in 1908 to solve a most baffling mystery: The British Museum is missing a specimen of a Martian from the failed invasion of 1899. Did it walk away on its own or did someone steal it?

Holmes ponders the facts and remembers his part in the war effort alongside Professor Challenger during the War of the Worlds invasion that was chronicled in H.G. Wells' classic novel.

Meanwhile, Doctor Watson has problems of his own when his wife steals a scalpel from his surgical tool kit and returns to her old stomping grounds of Whitechapel, the London

CALIBER PRESENTS

The original Caliber Presents anthology title was one of Caliber's inaugural releases and featured predominantly new creators, many of which went onto successful careers in the comic's industry. In this new version, Caliber Presents has expanded to graphic novel size and while still featuring new creators it also includes many established professional creators with new visions. Creators featured in this first issue include nominees and winners of some of the industry's major awards including the Eisner, Harvey, Xeric, Ghastly, Shel Dorf, Comic Monsters, and more.

LEGENDLORE

From Caliber Comics now comes the entire Realm and Legendlore saga as a set of volumes that collects the long running critically acclaimed series. In the vein of The Lord of The Rings and The Hobbit with elements of Game of Thrones and Dungeon and Dragons.

Four normal modern day teenagers are plunged into a world they thought only existed in novels and film. They are whisked away to a magical land where dragons roam the skies, orcs and hobgoblins terrorize travelers, where unicorns prance through the forest, and kingdoms wage war for dominance. It is a world where man is just one race, joining other races such as elves, trolls, dwarves, changelings, and the dreaded night creatures who steal the night.

TIME GRUNTS

What if Hitler's last great Super Weapon was – Time itself! A WWII/time travel adventure that can best be described as *Band of Brothers* meets *Time Bandits*.

October, 1944. Nazi fortunes appear bleaker by the day. But in the bowels of the Wenceslas Mines, a terrible threat has emerged . . . The Nazis have discovered the ability to conquer time itself with the help of a new ominous device!

Now a rag tag group of American GIs must stop this threat to the past, present, and future . . . While dealing with their own past, prejudices, and fears in the process.

CALIBER
C O M I C S

www.calibercomics.com